WHAT'S FOR DINNER, DEXTE

COOKING FOR YOUR DOG
USING CHINESE MEDICINE THEORY

By JUDY MORGAN D.V.M.

and TONYA WILHELM

WHAT'S FOR DINNER, DEXTER?

COOKING FOR YOUR DOG
USING CHINESE MEDICINE THEORY

ISBN-13: 978-1505890310

Printed in the United States of America

CONTENTS

Just the Slow Cooker

Move Over Slow Cooker

Meals to Go and Snacks

FEEDING DEXTER THE DOG

by "Mom"

Since July 2013, with the help of holistic veterinarian Dr. Judy Morgan, I have been home cooking for Dexter. Throughout this book, you will find some of our home cooked meals and recipes. This book is not intended to be a tell-all on how to cook for **your** dog; it is intended to be an inspiration for your own creations. Please keep in mind all dogs are different in their dietary needs. Before changing your dog's food regimen, please speak to your veterinarian. If your veterinarian is not well versed in home cooking or is against home cooking, seek out the advice of a holistic veterinarian.

In the beginning, Dexter's breeder fed him a raw diet. In a nutshell, a raw diet consists of raw meat, bones, vegetables, fruits, and minerals. There is, of course, more to it; but I personally have not done too much research on feeding raw. I just have not gotten to that point yet.

When Dexter joined our family as a puppy, I fed him a premium kibble recommended by his breeder, omega-rich eggs, cooked meats (salmon, beef, ground turkey, chicken breast and pork), fatty acids, and supplements. My long term goal was to home cook all of Dexter's meals from the beginning, but I was worried I would miss something in his nutritional needs. Then along came Dr. Judy Morgan and her pet food webinars! These informative webinars were just what I needed to get the ball rolling.

ABOUT ME
by Dexter the Dog

Thank you for your interest in my life; I am honored to have you join in my adventures! Some of you may be familiar with me already from my Facebook page and other social media outlets. But for my new friends, I will be writing about my healthy eating throughout this book. I do appreciate you taking time out of your day to visit with me.

My name is Dexter and I am a very happy cavalier King Charles spaniel. I was born on October 6, 2009. I had 3 brothers and 3 sisters. My favorite sibling is Lambeau; we still visit each other once in a while and chat on Facebook. He really is my buddy! For the first 5 weeks of my life I was cared for by a wonderful family. I had lots of aunties to take care of me and human companions too.

On November 15, 2009 a family came to visit us. They spent about 3 hours playing, holding and talking to me and my brothers. I immediately fell in love with them! I was especially fond of "Tonya" and did not want to leave her side. When the family left, I was sad to see them go, but Tonya said she would see me in about 6 weeks. She left a soft blanket for me to snuggle and play on.

December 19, 2009 was a very cold and snowy day. I could tell something was going on, as the human folks were buzzing around getting some bags and doggie car seats together. A nice family came by in the morning and loved on one of my sisters. We said our goodbyes and she went off to her new wonderful home.

THEN I SAW THEM! I knew they wouldn't let me down. Tonya and the rest of her family came to visit me again. Tonya spent another hour playing with Lambeau and me. She told me how happy she was to finally be able to take me to my new home, for a brand new adventure.

She told me I could call her "Mom."

2

THE BACK STORY

by "Mom"

As long as I can remember I have been in love with dogs. I never was your typical child loving their pet; I had more of a devotion and true admiration for other creatures. In my pre-toddler period we had various dogs that we cared for as a family. My mom had a soft spot in her heart for stray dogs and would readily bring them home, until a new forever home was found for them.

For my fifth birthday my parents said I could get a puppy of my own! Mom, Dad, and I hopped into the car and went to our local animal shelter where there were rows and rows of puppies and dogs to choose from. Then I saw him; a cute little buff colored dog, resembling a collie golden retriever mix. "Toby" would become my constant companion from that day until he crossed the rainbow bridge 12 years later.

Toby was my true friend through my childhood and he was with me during my parents' divorce. His passing was very traumatic for me and is still painful today. Unfortunately, after Toby's passing, we were not in a position to bring another dog into our family. I was heartbroken, to say the least.

High school came and went, as did college. At various times during my college years, I often thought about bringing a dog into my life. But, reason would kick in and I did not give in to my urges. I found other ways to get my doggie fix by answering pet sitting ads in the local paper.

In my final year of undergraduate school, studying fine arts, I realized I was not going down my true path. Instead of enrolling in a graduate program, I decided to take a position at the Columbus Zoo and Aquarium. I wasn't sure what I wanted to do with my life.

After a few months at the zoo, I realized I still had this void. I was yearning for the companionship I had lost. I took a kennel position at the Capital Area Humane Society in Columbus, Ohio. My void was starting to dissipate. But now I felt more sadness; there were so many animals without a forever home.

My manager advised me that, if I got my job done, I could spend the rest of my time walking the dogs. So I did. But I didn't just walk them, I started to train them. I would work with the dogs on confidence building skills, polite manners, and play. These seemed to be the areas where the dogs needed the most help.

But it still didn't seem like I was doing enough. What else could I do? Why did people drop off their dogs here? What could I do to prevent the dogs from getting to this point in the first place?

Training dogs and training dog parents seemed to be the logical solution. But where would I start? Luckily for me, there was an organization in my hometown, Assistance Dogs of America, that rescued Labrador and golden retrievers from local shelters and trained them to become service dogs for people with disabilities. And the best part, they were in need of volunteers!

Off I went. I took a paid position at South Suburban Animal Hospital, while volunteering at Assistance Dogs of America. It was definitely a win-win situation for me. I was in learning over-drive! My life became dogs 24/7 and I loved it. Finally, about a year after I started volunteering, Assistance Dogs of America was able to bring me on as a staff member. With the blessings of South Suburban's veterinarians and staff, I accepted my new role.

It was not long after starting my new position as staff dog trainer at Assistance Dogs of America that I moved into the apartment above the training center. The training center was set in the rural town of Swanton, Ohio, in a farm house with 2.5 acres of fenced-in land. The offices were downstairs and my new home was upstairs. Now my life would truly revolve around dogs, dog training and their behavior. On my days off, I would often take a service-dog-in-training with me on my errands. Sitting at my bedroom window watching the dogs in the yard interacting with each other was the highlight of my evenings.

But something was still missing from my life, a dog to call my very own. I needed a special friend that was devoted to me and me to him. To help fill that void, I would choose one dog from the training program to bring upstairs with me in the evenings. Another winning solution for both the dog and me, but it still wasn't the same as having a dog of my very own.

Then on December 19, 2000, it happened. The director received a phone call from Lenawee Humane Society saying they had found three golden retriever puppies roaming the cold winter fields of Ohio! She asked me if I wanted to adopt one...of course I said, "Yes!"

The puppies, Alvin, Simon, and Theodore, already weighed 30 pounds and were 3 months old. These boys seemed like your typical puppies: rambunctious, fun-loving, and peeing all the time! Because it was the week of Christmas, I was the only staff member taking care of the pups throughout the week, but I loved it! I couldn't think of a better way to spend my holiday.

On December 27, 2000, the director made her decision that Theodore, aka Theo, would become my very own! Finally, my void had been filled. A dog to love, take on adventures, become my demo dog, and my true companion day in and day out. Theo. I made a promise to him that day that I would do everything I could to help him have a wonderful, rich, and fulfilling life. I would do whatever I needed to ensure his safety and happiness from that point on.

Our first few months were pure bliss! Theo and I did everything together from demos, walks, public outings, playtime, to snuggle time. Unfortunately, things started to take a downward turn that summer. Theo started to develop issues with other dogs after an unfortunate event at a dog day care. He became unpredictable around the other dogs at the training center. So much so, that I soon realized I would need to move out if I wanted to help Theo relax.

So Theo and I packed up and moved. We really moved; to Raleigh, North Carolina! New behaviors started to sneak into Theo's routine: thunder phobia, separation anxiety, and eventually, generalized anxiety. I met with various dog trainers, consulted animal behaviorists, and even a veterinarian behaviorist. Our blissful existence was no more.

Theo's anxiety, especially with the daily thunderstorms, living 12 hours away from family, running my own pet sitting and dog training business, finally took its toll. In 2006, after Theo's sixth birthday, we moved back to Ohio to be with my family. This allowed Theo to have more companionship while I was out working and to suffer through fewer storms.

In September 2009 I came to the hard decision that Theo was not leading a good life. His anxieties got the better of him. Every day he was having a panic attack. It was so sad and heartbreaking; I felt that I had let him down. I still feel that way, even though I know in my heart I did everything humanly possible. Theo is in a better place now and sleeping peacefully. God bless my family for helping Theo and me those last 3 years.

MY ARRIVAL

by Dexter the Dog

When I arrived at my new home, I was shown a big toy box filled with lots of toys and chews. I had three big, soft beds around the house to jump in and hide deep inside the cushions. I couldn't believe all this was mine! There were so many fun things to look at and explore.

Then I saw them, two other animals that I had never seen before. They seemed pretty neat and friendly. Mom called them "Nutter" and "Cookie". Cookie and I became friends right away. She loved to run and play, just like me. Nutter needed some time to adjust to my silly puppy antics and energy.

I could tell life was going to be very good. I had Mom, Grandma, Eddie, Cookie, and Nutter to entertain me all day long. Mom would take me on daily adventures to different parks, pet stores, human schools, and even Bass Pro Shops! Eddie would always go on our adventures when we went to Bass Pro. He would always tell me I was the best dog ever!

About three times a week, Grandma would take me to "school" where Mom taught other doggies and their parents life skills. Going to school with Grandma is one of my favorite things to do. I really love spending one-on-one time with Grandma. I love her so much.

On the weekends the real fun happens. Mom, Grandma, Eddie, and I go on new adventures. You name it, we do it! Everything from picnics at parks, boat rides, fishing trips, dog walk fundraisers, yappy hours, local festivals, and even visiting a horse farm! The best part of our adventures is that we are all together as a family. That makes me really happy. As long as my family is together, I'm content. My weeks are full of adventures, and each summer we have great family vacations. Life is good and I know it.

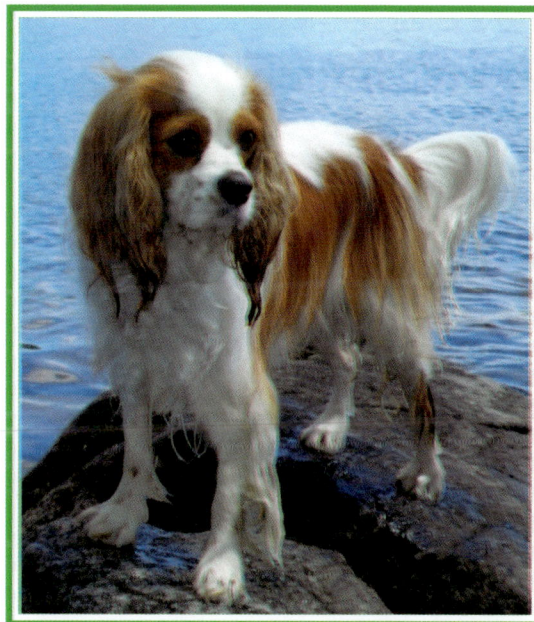

WHAT'S SO GREAT ABOUT HOME COOKING?

by Judy Morgan D.V.M.

I have been a practicing veterinarian for over thirty years. I used to believe that all pet foods were created equal and prescription diet pet foods were the only answer for pets suffering with chronic diseases. Luckily, I changed the course of my career about twenty years ago and became a holistic veterinary practitioner. I became enamored with the idea that "real" foods could be used to treat my patients. I love cooking for my pets and they certainly love to eat what I cook. Helping clients determine the best ingredients for their own pets is one of my biggest delights in practice.

I share cooking duties with my partner, Hue Grant. When we met, Hue was a "recreational" chef; he has since honed his skills and knows his way around the kitchen as well as many professionals. Hue is my partner in culinary creations and has been an inspiration for many of my recipes.

We do a lot of rescue work, trying to save dogs that are unwanted or abandoned. Many of the dogs we rescue have long term health issues. We have found that using food as therapy helps the dogs heal faster. It has taken quite a few years for us to feel really comfortable cooking for our dogs. Many veterinarians will tell pet owners it is impossible to feed a balanced home cooked meal. However, we have discovered that it is not impossible. Home cooking will take revenue away from your veterinarian who wants to sell prescription diets. But by following our recipes you will start to feel more comfortable cooking for your pets. Once you do, feel free to start adding in substitutions based on your pet's needs.

Home cooking became a way of life for many pet owners after the recalls of hundreds of brands of pet foods due to contamination with melamine which killed many pets, starting around 2005. Other pet owners want to cook because they want to control the ingredients fed to their pets. Animals with food allergies or food intolerances may need a restricted diet with novel proteins; diabetic pets need a diet low in carbohydrates; pets in kidney failure need diets with high quality, restricted protein levels. Although many restricted-ingredient diets are now entering the pet food market, it may be difficult to find a product with the exact ingredients that may be needed. Some pets do not do well on any processed products and thrive on raw or home cooked diets.

Recalls due to contamination with bacteria like salmonella and fungal elements like aspergilla have scared off many pet owners who previously fed processed products. People have become infected with salmonella and died after handling contaminated processed dry kibble and canned pet food products. This is not a common problem, but always makes the headlines and scares the rest of the population.

The pet-owner bond is strengthened when owners feel they are contributing to their pet's well-being and good health on one of the most intimate levels of human bonding: food. How many mothers encourage their children to eat more to grow strong and healthy? We have the same bond with our pets, using food as rewards. I know our dogs and cats crowd around the kitchen whenever we cook, but particularly when they see us grinding meat or getting out the slow cooker, which almost always means food for them. Even grabbing a morsel that drops to the floor or getting a small handout during the cooking process is reason for celebration.

HOW DO I START?

So how do you start cooking for your pet? The easiest method of home cooking is accomplished using a slow cooker. They come in all shapes and sizes and prices. We happen to own one of the biggest slow cookerss available because we are always cooking for a huge gang. Depending on the size of the slow cooker and the number of animals being fed, enough meals can be made for a week or more in one pot. Anything that can be fed within two to three days can be stored in the refrigerator. Anything that will not be used within a few days can be stored in multiple or single-serving containers in the freezer and defrosted as needed. Another easy way to prepare meals is by making baked meat loafs, varying ingredients as needed. Meals do not have to be complicated and should incorporate ingredients your pet likes and needs. Meals can be designed to treat different diseases, as will be discussed in upcoming chapters.

The hardest part of home cooking for pets is achieving a balanced meal that includes a healthy complement of vitamins and minerals. It is difficult to achieve the levels of calcium that animals require in home cooked meals, so it is always important to add a calcium supplement. Dehydrated, ground eggshells can be added to the diet to provide calcium, but I prefer a balanced mineral supplement made for home cooking, which will also include trace minerals. My preferred product is Rx Minerals, made by Rx Vitamins. This product was formulated specifically for owners who wanted to cook for their pets after the melamine scare of 2005. If eggshell is being used, the average content of calcium is about 500 mg per half teaspoon of finely ground shell. That amount of eggshell should be added to every pound of food that is fed. The other vitamin that is hard to provide in adequate amounts is Vitamin D. Vitamin D is found in eggs and fish in high quantities, but recipes that do not incorporated these ingredients should be supplemented at the rate of 25 IU per pound of pet's body weight.

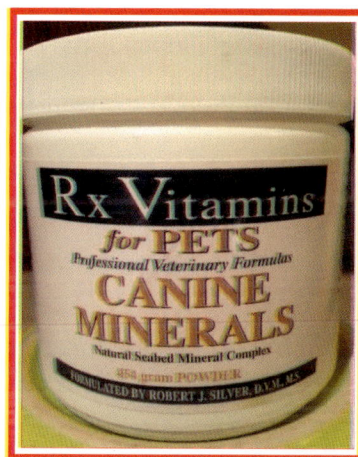

Knowing how much food to feed also becomes a dilemma for owners making their own pet food. Pets will consume an average of two to three percent of their body weight per day, depending on activity level, age, lifestyle, and breed. Larger breeds tend to need a lower percentage than smaller breeds. Very active or energetic pets will need a higher percentage. The weight of the food can be extremely variable, depending on the amount of liquid in the diet. Some pets like their food nice and soupy, while others will prefer the food to be drier.

Another way to determine the amount to feed is by knowing the approximate number of calories your pet needs. Most dogs require 20 to 30 calories per pound of body weight per day; again, depending on breed, age, lifestyle, and activity level. The easiest way to determine the correct amount to feed is to make an educated guess based on calories and percentage of body weight, then start feeding that amount and weigh your pet in two weeks. If there is unwanted weight gain or loss, adjust your feeding accordingly. Home cooking is actually one of the easiest ways for pets to achieve weight loss because owners can easily control the amount of calories fed.

Examples of math to figure out how much to feed using % body weight:

20 pound dog, moderate activity level. Using average 2% of body weight:

0.02 x 20 pounds = 0.4 pounds of food

0.4 pounds x 16 ounces per pound of food = 6.4 ounces of food per day

Split into two meals, so approximately 3.2 ounces should be fed twice daily.

50 pound dog, trains daily for agility. Using average 3% of body weight:

0.03 x 50 pounds = 1.5 pounds of food

1.5 x 16 ounces per pound of food = 24 ounces of food per day

Split into two meals, so approximately 12 ounces should be fed twice daily.

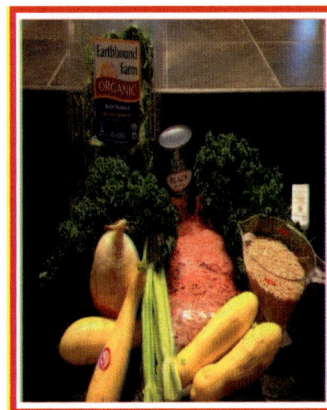

Examples of math to figure out how much to feed using calories:

20 pound dog, moderate activity level. Using 25 calories per pound of body weight:

20 pounds x 25 calories per pound = 500 calories per day

Split into two meals, so approximately 250 calories per meal.

50 pound dog, trains daily for agility. Using 30 calories per pound of body weight:

50 pounds x 30 calories = 1500 calories per day

Split into two meals, so approximately 750 calories per meal.

All dogs (and cats) should be fed twice daily. Take the amount of food required and split into two equal meals fed close to twelve hours apart. Use the guidelines above as *guidelines.* Adjust up or down based on body condition.

It is extremely important to vary the diet that you feed your pet. Just as deficiencies can occur when feeding the same processed food day in and day out, the same problem exists with home-made diets. Be sure to rotate proteins, vegetables, grains, beans, and herbs to achieve an overall balance over time.

SOME THINGS TO AVOID

Certain foods should be avoided when cooking for your pets, as they may be toxic to pets.

FOODS THAT MAY BE TOXIC TO PETS

Chocolate – contains theobromine which can cause hyperactivity, seizures, rapid heart rate, death

Macadamia Nuts – vomiting, weakness, tremors, drunken walk, death

Grapes and Raisins – vomiting, diarrhea, kidney failure, death; not all dogs are susceptible

Apricot, peach, cherry, plum pits – contain cyanide, cause vomiting, shock, cardiac arrest, death

Onions – hemolytic anemia, vomiting, diarrhea, bloody urine; effects of eating onions are cumulative

Green tomatoes, tomato vines and leaves – vomiting, diarrhea, seizures

Scallions – hemolytic anemia, vomiting, diarrhea, bloody urine, death

Raw and green potatoes – vomiting, diarrhea, seizures, heart arrhythmias

Rhubarb – tremors, seizures, heart arrhythmias, kidney disease, high in oxalates

Nutmeg – tremors, muscle spasms, seizures, death

Persimmon seeds – vomiting, diarrhea, fever

Raw dough or yeast – produces ethanol, causes liver failure, seizures, drunken gait, coma, death

Alcohol – depression, weakness, liver failure, coma, death

Raw salmon or trout – can carry a parasite that causes salmon poisoning. Canned or cooked is okay.

Avocado Peel – vomiting, diarrhea, fluid accumulation

Some internet sites will also list foods like garlic, mushrooms, walnuts, almonds, and liver as being toxic to pets. While garlic can cause hemolytic anemia when fed in large quantities, it also has many beneficial effects. It has antibacterial, antifungal, and antiviral effects, as well as being a good Yang tonic, transforms Phlegm, drains Damp, and resolves stagnation. The key is quantity fed. One clove per twenty pounds body weight daily should be a safe level to feed.

Some mushrooms, like Shiitake, Maitake, and Reishi, have anti-cancer effects, as well as draining Damp.

Liver is high in vitamin A and is also the filtering organ for the body. Organic or grass-fed, hormone-free, antibiotic-free liver should be used and liver should not be fed in large quantities every day.

Black walnuts can cause liver damage. Other nuts, particularly walnuts, pecans, pistachios, and Brazil nuts, may be contaminated with aflatoxins, which can cause liver failure. The aflatoxin is usually found in the hulls, not the nut itself.

Cruciferous vegetables are very healthy, but can suppress thyroid function if fed raw in large amounts. Since they are hard to digest, they should be finely chopped or cooked. These include broccoli, cauliflower, brussel sprouts, cabbage, arugula, bok choy, kale, collard greens, mustard greens, turnips, watercress, rutabaga, daikon, and kohlrabi. Spinach and swiss chard are high in oxalates and should only be fed in small amounts or not at all if you have a pet prone to oxalate stones or crystals in the urine. Certain small breed dogs like yorkies, maltese, and bichons seem to be more susceptible.

White potatoes, tomatoes, peppers, and eggplant belong to the nightshade family and contain a substance called solanine. Solanine may aggravate arthritis pain and other inflammatory conditions. This does not occur in all individuals who eat these vegetables, only those who are sensitive to the solanine.

WHAT'S REALLY IN PROCESSED DOG FOOD?

Many of you may wonder why we would go to the trouble of writing a cookbook for dogs. The answer to that question is easy, once you know what's really in the processed foods available for pets. For years, we both fed processed foods to our animals, but somewhere along the way, we discovered the true meaning of the ingredients incorporated into those pet foods and decided we could no longer feed our animals those products. We have discovered some products that we feel are high enough quality to feed our beloved pets, but there are many that are too horrible to ever cross the thresholds of our doors. In order for you to understand the need for wholesome, fresh foods for your pets, it is important to know what you should *not* be feeding.

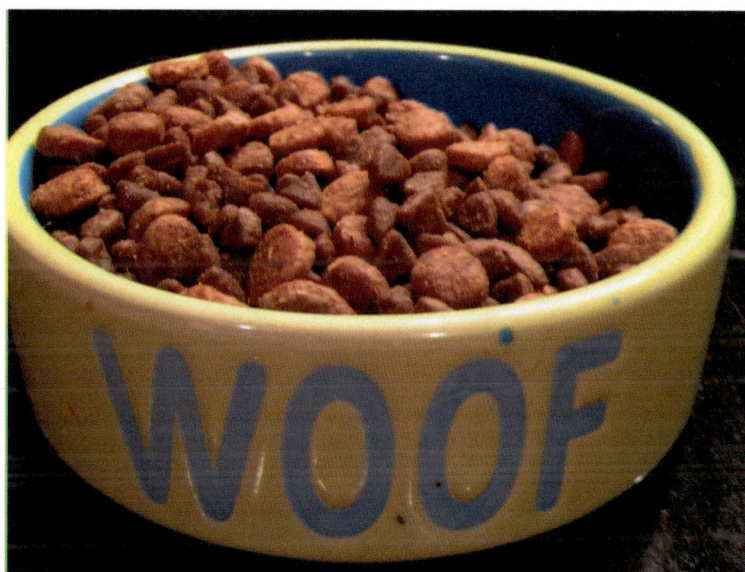

What constitutes *real* food? Anything grown in a field, whether plant or animal, may be considered real food. However, with the advent of genetically modified grains, even foods that we would normally consider "natural" have possibly become toxic. Certainly, the genetically modified foods that are engineered to produce larger crops have had a significant impact on insect species that are important contributors to life on this planet. Raising livestock in high density, confinement operations, with added antibiotics, hormones, and steroids to promote rapid growth has completely changed the taste and healthy status of the meats we eat. Farm raised fish are being fed genetically modified grains which may impact the meat we eat from those fish.

Most pet owners are not aware of the origins of most of the ingredients used to make processed pet foods. They take solace when reading package labeling that proclaims the food meets or exceeds the requirements of AAFCO (Association of American Feed Control Officials), which sounds very legitimate. But these requirements may not be the 'Golden Seal of Approval' that pet food manufacturers make them out to be.

AAFCO feeding trials consist of at least eight dogs being fed the same diet for a mere 26 weeks (approximately six months). During this time, 25% of the dogs (two animals) can be removed from the test and the dogs eating the food can lose up to 15% of their weight and condition, with only a few blood parameters measured. As long as the remaining dogs in the trial appear healthy and have acceptable weights and certain blood values, the food passes and is considered 'complete and balanced' nutrition for whatever life stage it was tested (puppy, adult maintenance, senior, etc.). So it can now be fed to your pet for a period much longer than the six-month test period. Just about any diet with a modicum of protein, fat, and carbohydrates, from any source, could keep pets alive for this period of time and fulfill those conditions. But if you consider that pets may be fed this diet for a lifetime, you will see a much bigger problem. Losing 15% of body weight in six months could be a death sentence over a lifetime.

AAFCO feeding trials were not designed to measure the long-term effects of commercial diets. AAFCO trials were designed to ensure that pet foods were not harmful to the animal and would support the proposed life stage for a period of only 26 weeks. The AAFCO protocols were not designed to examine nutritional relationships to long-term health or disease prevention. If a dog lives for six months with no noticeable ill effects while eating a kibble, then the food is considered 100% complete and balanced nutrition, even though long-term nutritional deficiencies may occur several years down the road. This is one of the reasons I have always recommended a rotational diet if you feed processed foods. Hopefully, over the course of time, you will fulfill the nutritional needs of your pets and avoid deficiencies and effects of toxins present in one diet formulation.

In addition to the AAFCO statement, there are many other misunderstood terms on pet food labels. The term "natural" means anything found in animal, plant, or mineral form in nature that is not chemically synthesized. However, *natural* products can be chemically processed and still be considered natural. Not all things that are *natural* are healthy. After all, rattlesnake venom and arsenic are natural, but that doesn't mean we would want those ingredients included in the food we eat or feed to our pets. Don't be fooled by the word *natural* when used to name a pet food, because it really does not equate to *healthy.*

Other misleading terms used to name pet foods include the words *organic* or *made with organic ingredients*. Unfortunately, those terms are really not regulated in the pet food industry, but our hope is that pet food manufacturers follow the guidelines set out in the human food industries. In order for a food to be labeled *organic*, 95% of the ingredients used to make the food must be raised organically. If a label states "made with organic ingredients", between seventy and ninety five percent of the ingredients must be raised or cultivated organically. If the product contains less than seventy percent organic ingredients, each organic ingredient can be listed individually.

The terms *premium, holistic,* and *human-grade* have no legal definitions in the pet food industry, so any manufacturer can use those terms in pet food labeling. Consumers are easily fooled into thinking they are buying a superior product when, in reality, they may be buying a product made with very inferior ingredients.

When a label names the product as *dinner, platter, formula, entrée, or recipe,* the food need only contain 24% to 95% of that ingredient. So a food labeled as *Beef Formula* may only contain 24% beef. A product labeled *with* contains anywhere from 3% to 24% of the labeled ingredient. When looking for a product that is high in meat, for instance, these products will be very low in meat, containing mostly fillers as the other 76% of the diet. Products labeled *flavor,* as in *beef flavored,* do not actually contain any of the named ingredient. Something that is *flavored* only tastes like the named ingredient, which may be accomplished using chemical ingredients to make the flavor.

Cats are carnivores and must eat meat to remain healthy. Dogs are omnivores or carnivores, depending on who you ask, and are much healthier when fed meat, so pet food products should have high meat content. Meat provides protein in the diet (although there are many artificial ways to elevate protein content in food).

Meat products can be listed in many different ways on pet food labels. The AAFCO definition of chicken falls under Poultry; duck and turkey would have the same definitions. The AAFCO definition states poultry is a combination of flesh and skin and could include bone. The definition does not include feathers, heads, feet or entrails of the animals. The poultry/chicken in pet food does not have to be USDA inspected and approved; specifically stated in the definition as *"suitable for use in animal food".* This ingredient could consist of almost 100% chicken/poultry meat or it could consist of less than 1% meat, 99% skin and bone, or it could be somewhere in-between. The definition allows for any variation in pet food while still being labeled as chicken. Chicken can be a high quality ingredient if it includes meat, not just skin and bones, and is sourced from chicken that has been USDA inspected and approved. Note this does not mean the facility has been inspected. You can have a USDA facility that has been inspected, but the meat itself may not have been inspected.

The official definition of poultry does not include the requirement it must be sourced from slaughtered animals. This ingredient can include animals that have died prior to slaughter, such as euthanized animals and/or animals that have died in the field or during transport. Chicken by-product meal (poultry by-product meal) and chicken by-product (poultry by-product) definitions do include the requirement that sourcing must be from slaughtered animals.

By-product meal is a dehydrated product made from the feet, necks, undeveloped eggs, intestines, and internal organs like heart, liver, gizzard, and kidneys of slaughtered animals. It does not contain muscle meat fit for human consumption. If specified as chicken, turkey, beef, etc., the by-product comes only from that animal. If the label states *meat* by-product the source can be any animal, including the by-products from diseased, dead, dying, and decayed animals not fit for human consumption. No usable muscle meat is included in any by-products.

Meat meal, on the other hand, is a ground, rendered (cooked) ingredient that can include muscle meat, skin and bone. It does not include chicken/poultry heads, feathers, feet or entrails. This provides a more concentrated source of protein, however it has been more highly processed. I would not eliminate a food from my feeding regimen just because a specific meat meal was the first ingredient, as this can be a high quality ingredient. Notice I said *specific meat meal,* by which I mean chicken, turkey, beef, etc. Unnamed "meat" can include rendered product from any mammal tissue, which can include 4-D meat according to AAFCO guidelines. Four-D stands for dead, dying, decayed, and diseased; these are the meats that are not allowed to enter the human food chain. This is the worst of the worst and testing of 4-D meat has shown euthanasia solution to be present in most batches of meat meal. We are feeding our pets euthanasia solution on a daily basis. How horrid.

The same guidelines are used when feeding a fish-based food. The type of fish should be specifically named, like sardines, salmon, or whitefish. Generic fishmeal can contain waste products that are not healthy. Fishmeal can also be preserved with Ethoxyquin, a chemical that is used as a pesticide and for making rubber; it is known to cause changes in the liver and kidneys. Ethoxyquin will not be listed on the ingredient label if the chemical was added prior to the arrival of the fishmeal at the pet food manufacturing plant.

Animal Digest is another awful ingredient commonly found in lower quality foods and in some products like probiotic supplements. Animal digest is made of chemically treated animal tissue. The animal tissue is not specified and can come from 4-D animals. Chemicals are being added to the meat to "digest" it and we are feeding it to our pets. Animal digest is commonly added to inferior products to artificially raise the protein content of the food.

Animal Fat is obtained from the tissues of mammals and/or poultry in the commercial process of rendering or extracting. Animal fat is a byproduct of meat meal processing. The origin of the contributing animals is never known, and may include road-kill, dead zoo animals, euthanized animals, and 4-D animals. The resulting oil is very low in linoleic acid - an essential fatty acid that is important for skin and coat health. Animal fat is commonly preserved with carcinogenic chemicals like BHA, BHT, and Ethoxyquin.

Meat and bone meal is added to pet food as another way to artificially elevate protein content. As defined by AAFCO, meat and bone meal is the rendered product from animal tissues, including bone. Rendering is the process by which an entire carcass, excluding the edible meat for human consumption, is cooked down and dehydrated to make a meal. In Europe, the vast majority of meat and bone meal is used as a fossil fuel replacement for renewable energy generation, and as a fuel in cement kilns, landfilling or incineration. For years, advocates of home cooking for pets have used bone meal as a calcium supplement for home cooked diets. I recommend not using this product, as it is made from poor quality ingredients and may come from 4-D animals.

Many pet owners have gravitated toward "grain-free" diets in the past few years, believing that all grains are bad for animals. This is not necessarily true and many grains are healthy additives for some pets. When reading pet food labels it is important to understand what the ingredients actually contain. *Ground corn* includes the entire ear of corn ground, without husks, including the cob. Whole ground wheat, rice, or barley include the hulls as well as the grain kernels. These can be an important source of fiber in the diet, but can also be used as undigestible fillers that contribute little to the caloric needs of the pet. Corn, soy, and wheat have often been blamed for pet allergies. These are not necessarily digested well by dogs and cats and don't deserve a place in pet diets in large quantities, yet many pet foods rely heavily on these ingredients, including some very high-priced diets.

Sugars including high fructose corn syrup, sucrose, maltodextrose, and others have no place in pet food. Animals have no need for sugar in their diet and these contribute to obesity and diabetes, just as in the human food industry. Sugars are added as flavor enhancers in poor quality foods and can also act as preservatives to make food last longer.

Preservatives including Ethoxyquin, BHA, and BHT have all been shown to be carcinogenic and should never be fed, even though they are commonly found in many lower quality pet foods on the market. Their use has been banned in many countries, but their use is still allowed in pet food in the United States. Artificial colors, dyes, and flavors are also added to entice the pet owner to buy low quality foods. The animals can't tell the differences in the colors and don't really care. High quality food manufacturers will never add these potentially carcinogenic ingredients to their products.

Corn or rice gluten meals are by-products of the human food industry; they are the dried residue after the removal of most of the starch and germ. These are used as fillers to boost the protein level in the food. Gluten meals are a common source of allergies in pets and I will not use a food containing any sort of gluten.

Canned pet foods usually contain some sort of binder or thickening agent. Carrageenan, which is extracted from red seaweed, has been implicated as a carcinogen. Guar gum, xanthan gum, cellulose gum, wheat gluten, corn gluten, and rice gluten are other binders commonly used. They are a poor protein source, have minimal nutritional value, and can contribute to allergies and inflammatory bowel disease. Some of the high end pet food companies have stopped using these products, but they are now adding potato starch, pea starch, or tapioca as binders. Some pets are now developing allergies and intolerances to these binding agents.

Powdered cellulose is purified, mechanically disintegrated cellulose prepared by processing alpha cellulose obtained as a pulp from fibrous plant materials. Powdered cellulose is a fancy term for wood. Dried wood is cleaned and processed into a fine powder and used to add bulk and consistency to cheap pet foods.

Brewer's rice is another ingredient used as a filler; it is added to artificially boost protein levels in food. This is a by-product of the brewing industry from making wort or beer and has very little nutrient value. Brewer's Yeast is also a waste product of the brewing industry. It is used for flavoring, protein, and B-vitamins. This product can become very toxic to the liver and causes allergies and arthritis.

You might ask why so many products are added to pet food to artificially raise the protein levels in the diets. This is done because AAFCO has issued guidelines stating the minimum levels of protein in pet foods for different life stages. Rather than use expensive, high quality meat products, it is much more economically rewarding for the pet food companies to use lower priced, lower quality ingredients to artificially raise protein levels. Unfortunately, the dilemma of raising protein levels also lead to the introduction of melamine into the pet food industry around the world and the dairy industry in China. Many pets and humans died when tainted products were introduced into the food chain, resulting in many pet owners scrambling to make balanced homemade diets for their pets.

Pet food manufacturers have gotten wise to the fact that people are looking for more wholesome ingredients in pet food. They have started advertising foods with added fruits and vegetables; they are making attractive labels with pictures of fruits and vegetables. The ingredients are listed in order of abundance on the label. If you find cranberries, blueberries, and other fruits and vegetables at the end of the list, be assured there are only a few bits of those fruits and vegetables in the bag or can. It's a great advertising gimmick, but it isn't doing anything beneficial for your pet. A general rule of thumb is that any ingredient listed after salt on the ingredient list is not present in a significant amount and your pet is not getting any benefit from those ingredients.

THE ENERGETICS OF FOOD

Yin and Yang are complementary opposites which are the Chinese principles that govern balance in life. Without a balance of Yin and Yang life would cease to exist. A deficiency or excess of either principle will result in an imbalance. Imbalance results in disease. For instance, an excess of Yang, which is heat, results in fever. An excess of Yin, which is moisture, can lead to an accumulation of fluids in the body. The nature of Yin and Yang is not static, as each flows into the other like day flows into night. We encounter examples of Yin and Yang every day as we go through life. Nothing is completely Yin and nothing is completely Yang. Everything has a bit of Yin or a bit of Yang as each aspect contains the beginning point of the other aspect. They are interdependent on each other. As one aspect increases, the other decreases, to maintain overall balance of the whole.

CHARACTERISTICS OF YIN	CHARACTERISTICS OF YANG
Cold	Hot
Night	Day
Down	Up
Inside	Outside
Bottom	Top
Earth	Sky
Heavy	Light
Wet	Dry
Female	Male
Old	Young
Slow	Fast
Negative	Positive
Black/dark	White/bright
Soft	Hard
Weak	Strong
Passive	Dominate
Still	Active
Small	Large
Quiet	Loud
Right	Left
Salty, sour, bitter	Pungent, sweet
Blue, purple, black	Red, yellow, white
Water	Fire
Short	Tall
North (in the northern hemisphere)	South (in the northern hemisphere)

All food can be classified as being more Yin or more Yang and will have an effect on the body when eaten. It will either warm or cool the body. Hot soup on a cold day will warm the body from the inside. Ice cream or watermelon on a hot day will cool the body. It is not only the temperature of the food when it is eaten that contributes to warming and cooling effects. The food itself is energetically charged as either cooling or warming. Food can make the body shiver or it can make the body sweat (except dogs and cats cannot sweat, so they will pant). You may not always feel the energetic action of the food that dramatically, but changes are occurring whether you feel them or not.

Why does it matter what effect food has on the body? The effects of Yin, or cooling, foods can be used to treat fevers and infections by cooling the body. Yin, or cooling, foods can be fed during the heat and humidity of summer to keep pets more comfortable. Yang, or warming, foods can be used to warm the body on cold days or in pets suffering from internal deficiencies. Food can also be used to temper certain behaviors in pets. A hyperactive Jack Russell terrier can be fed cooling foods to help "put out the fire" of their hyperactivity. A sluggish, overweight Labrador retriever can be fed warming foods to "rev the engine" and get him moving.

Many things can have an impact on the energetics of food. All food has an inherent energetic pattern, but how the food is raised, how it is processed, and the amount of moisture in the food, will all affect the energy given to the body when the food is eaten.

When feeding processed foods, dry food will be warmer energetically than canned food because dry food is cooked at higher temperatures and is more highly processed; canned food, which is generally cooked at low heat, will be warmer than processed commercial raw food. When feeding home-prepared foods, grilled foods will be hotter energetically than broiled foods. Moving down from there in order of decreasing heat: baked, steamed, slow-cooked, and lastly, raw foods would be energetically the coolest.

How a food ingredient is grown will also affect the energetics. Wild-caught, cold water fish will have a cooling nature, while farm-raised fish will have a warmer nature because they are fed corn and other grain products instead of the natural diet found in the ocean. Grass-fed, pasture raised beef and pork will be more cooling than feedlot-raised, corn-fed beef and pork. Meats that are processed from the slaughter of young animals will tend to have more warming energy than meats processed from the slaughter of older animals. Grains and vegetables that are processed when they are high in moisture will be more cooling than grains and vegetables that are processed after they are allowed to dry on the stalk or vine. The amount of moisture in the food will affect the energetics: the higher the moisture, the more cooling the food will be to the body.

ENERGETICS OF FOOD

COOLING FOODS (YIN TONICS)

MEATS: turkey, duck, cod, clams, rabbit, alligator, shark, egg whites, clam, mussel, conch, duck eggs, frog, herring, oyster, scallop, white fish, octopus

GRAINS and SEEDS: millet, barley, brown rice, buckwheat, chrysanthemum, flax seed, sesame seed, soybean oil, wheat, tofu

VEGETABLES and HERBS: alfalfa, spinach, broccoli, celery, tomato, mushroom, kelp, seaweed, cucumber, eggplant, tomato, radish, Mung bean, asparagus

FRUITS & NUTS: melons, pear, banana, strawberry, orange, mango, apple, blueberry, kiwi, persimmon, honey

WARMING FOODS (YANG TONICS)

MEATS: lamb, goat, venison, shrimp, pheasant, chicken, kangaroo, egg yolks, beef kidney, chicken liver, lamb kidney, lamb liver, lobster

GRAINS and SEEDS: oats, white rice, sorghum, quinoa, sunflower seed

VEGETABLES and HERBS: ginger, cinnamon, dill seed, rosemary, squash, pumpkin, peppers, basil, chestnuts, chives, cloves, coriander, fennel, ginger, garlic, hawthorn, horseradish, nutmeg, sweet potato, thyme, turmeric

FRUITS & NUTS: peach, apricot, citrus peel, coconut, papaya, blackberry, raspberry, cherry, tangerine, walnuts

NEUTRAL FOODS (can also be slightly warm or cool)

MEATS: pork, pork kidney, pork liver, quail, salmon (depending on how it is raised), whole chicken eggs, tripe, beef (depending on how it is raised), beef liver, bison, goose, jellyfish, carp, cuttlefish, eel, tuna, sardines, catfish, squid, trout

GRAINS & SEEDS: corn, sweet jasmine rice, beans (soy, green, string, black, broad, kidney, red), black sesame seeds, green peas

VEGETABLES & HERBS: peas, yam, cabbage, potato, sweet potato, carrots, cauliflower, radish, Shiitake mushrooms

FRUITS & NUTS: apples, dates, pineapple, longan, lotus, figs, lemon, lychee

I realize this sounds confusing and complicated, but once you understand the basics it gets a lot easier. So how do you decide whether your pet needs to be warmed or cooled? There are a lot of hints you can get from your pets. Very few people really pay attention to the color of their pets' tongues, but now is the time to start taking notice. If your pet has a pale, wet tongue, you need to add warming foods. If your pet has a dark red, dry tongue, he is too hot and needs cooling foods. If the coat and skin are dry and flaky, add cooling, moisturizing foods.

Pets with red hair generally tend to be hotter in nature and may benefit from cooling foods, whereas black hair tends to signify coolness and black pets may need more warming foods. Pets with dry, brittle foot pads and noses probably need foods that are cooling and moisturizing.

Pets that are very high-energy, like terriers and young animals, are generally hot and can benefit from being fed cooling foods. Feeding energetically "hot" foods like lamb or venison to a young Jack Russell terrier is like throwing paper on fire. The food will keep stoking the fire, but eventually the fire will burn out. The water system of the body will wear out (the kidneys) because the body keeps trying to put out the fire. By feeding high moisture, cooling foods over the lifetime of the "hot" animal, the water system of the body will be spared, resulting in a longer, healthier life. Sedentary pets can benefit from warming foods, which may give them more energy to get them up and moving.

Your pet's breed in relation to climate can also give you clues on what to feed. Alaskan breeds of dogs living in hot climates will suffer if fed warming foods. They are already too hot for the location where they live, so they will benefit greatly by being fed cooling food. Hairless breeds like the Chinese crested or Mexican breeds like the Chihuahua need warming foods (and a few sweaters) if they live in a cold environment. You can also get a hint by looking at what they might eat in their natural environment. Alaskan dogs may be fed wild caught ocean fish, which are cooling in nature. Mexican dogs might be fed goat or chicken, both of which are warming foods and would be a more natural diet for them.

The amount of water your pet drinks will also tell you how to change the diet. Pets that are hot and dry will drink a lot, while those who are cool and moist will drink very little. Thirst level will also depend on type of food being fed. Pets fed dry kibble will always drink more than pets fed high-moisture diets like stew or fresh raw food. Pets that live their lives being fed dry kibble are basically in a constant state of dehydration, always trying to replace the moisture missing from their diet.

The environment your pet chooses will also give you clues as to whether they are hot or cold. Pets that love to be outside in the snow, seek cool tile on which to sleep, or pant a lot are too hot and need to be fed cooling foods. Pets that love to lie outside on a sunny day, snuggle under the covers close to your body, and follow the sun's rays in the house looking for places to sleep are animals that are cold and need to be fed warming foods.

The age of your pet may also give you clues. Younger pets tend to be more energetic and have more heat in their bodies, benefiting from cooling foods. Older pets tend to be slower and have less heat, benefiting from warming foods. However, some older pets have used up all their cooling abilities from being fed processed dry kibble for a lifetime, so if they are hot and panting they will need cooling foods.

DETERMINING ENERGETICS OF YOUR PET

HOT PET (TOO YANG)

Pants a lot

Sleeps on cold tile floors

Does not like to snuggle very much or will get down after a few minutes of snuggling

Loves to play outside in the snow or on cold days

Is very active or restless

Usually young pets are hot, but old pets that have used up their cooling abilities can be hot

Pets with red, white, or yellow coats

Pets who have eaten dry kibble most of their life

Red, dry tongue

Dry, brittle foot pads, nose, and coat

Drinks excessively

COLD PET (TOO YIN)

Does not pant much

Sleeps under the covers

Loves to snuggle and enjoys body warmth

Loves to sleep outside in the sun on hot days

Is sluggish

Older pets (unless they have a Yin Deficiency - will pant and drink a lot and have dry nose, coat, pads if they are hot)

Pets with black or gray coats

Pets who eat very high moisture diets may become cold

Pale, wet tongue

Wet, drippy nose

Drinks very little

When determining the energetics of your pets, remember they may not have every characteristic on one side of the list. They may have some from each side; even though they may have excess Yang, they will still have some Yin. Choose foods based on the majority of the signs pointing to the condition they have. The key to feeding is BALANCE. Even if you decide your pet is hot, it is not desirable to feed only cooling foods. Over time it is possible make a "hot" pet cold by feeding too many cooling foods. It is also possible to make a "cold" pet hot by feeding too many warming foods. When making a diet for your pet choose the majority of ingredients based on the energetics you are trying to achieve, but add a few ingredients outside that energetic category to balance the meal.

WHAT'S THE FUSS ABOUT QI?

Qi (pronounced "chee") is the vital life source. It is energy. It regulates spiritual, mental, emotional, and physical balance. It is influenced by the opposing forces of Yin and Yang. **To make an appropriate response to the ever shifting dynamics of Yin and Yang, there must be a sufficient amount of Qi. It is impossible to have excess Qi.** Since most of the Qi used in life is extracted from the food we eat and the air we breathe, Chinese medicine places considerable importance upon an adequate and appropriate diet of fresh, high quality food, and the opportunity and ability to breathe good, clean air. Feed your pets well and don't smoke around them (after all, they really have no choice in the matter).

Where is Qi used in the body? Every organ has different functions. Kidney Qi is responsible for cleansing the body and supporting bones and growth. It also produces bone marrow and brain tissue and supports memory. Kidney Qi governs reproduction and a deficiency of Kidney Qi will result in infertility. The Kidneys govern the ears, so when Kidney Qi diminishes with age, hearing will decline and deafness will result. Diminishing Kidney Qi will cause hind end weakness, arthritis, and back pain. The final loss of Kidney Qi results in kidney failure and death.

Liver Qi is responsible for storing blood, nourishing and supporting tendons and ligaments, and keeps the eyes healthy. Weak Liver Qi usually results in stagnation, causing emotional outbursts and anger. Weak tendons and ligaments, resulting in anterior cruciate ligament tears, are commonly seen when Liver Blood and Qi deficiency occur. Liver Qi stagnation will cause reddening of the eyes, glaucoma, and conjunctivitis. A painful abdomen on palpation can be the result of Liver Qi stagnation.

Spleen Qi is responsible for transporting and transforming nutrients that are eaten to form nutrient Qi. (The Spleen in Chinese medicine is considered as a digestive organ, not the spleen we think of in Western medicine. People and animals that have had the spleen removed still have the digestive functions of the Chinese Spleen.) Spleen Qi regulates digestion, supports muscles, holds blood in the vessels, and holds organs in the body. Weak Spleen Qi will result in fatigue and lethargy, muscle weakness, diarrhea, indigestion, loss of appetite, fluid build-up like edema or ascites (fluid in the abdomen), and prolapse of organs (rectal, uterine, vaginal).

The Chinese Spleen does not like cold, so feeding too many energetically cold foods will damage the Spleen function. If the Spleen function has been damaged and there is too much moisture present (ascites – fluid in the abdomen, edema of the limbs, fluid in the lungs, watery diarrhea) the condition is called Dampness. Damp is any pathological accumulation of fluid or fat in the body. It is caused by feeding too many raw, cold, sweet, or mucous-forming foods. Sugar, yeast, wheat, saturated fats, roasted peanuts, dairy products, bread, pork, bananas, and concentrated juices are all foods that can lead to dampness when eaten in excess. If dampness becomes a problem, you can add foods that will drain the damp from the body. These include alfalfa, barley, celery, corn, garlic, horseradish, kidney beans, lemon, marjoram, mushroom, radish, rye, or turnips. If the Spleen function is too cold you can warm the Spleen by feeding venison, lamb, kidney, shrimp, lobster, chives, cinnamon, cloves, nutmeg, ginger, garlic, dill seed, fennel seed, basil, rosemary, thyme, or raspberries. The key to feeding is BALANCE, so feed a mixture of cooling, warming, and neutral foods to avoid too much cold and damp.

Lung Qi is responsible for breathing and respiration, voice, sweating, and sending fluids to the kidneys. Weak Lung Qi will result in breathlessness, weak voice, and spontaneous sweating. Lung Qi is also responsible for sending nutrients to the hair to produce bright pigmentation. Loss of pigmentation of the nose can be a sign of weak Lung Qi.

Stomach Qi is responsible for digestion and sending food and fluids down to the intestines. Abnormal Stomach Qi is usually rebellious Stomach Qi, resulting in vomiting or food being sent up instead of down. This will also result in a loss of appetite.

Heart Qi is responsible for moving blood and for controlling emotions. The heart houses the "Shen" which is the emotional control of the body. Anxiety, restlessness, and insomnia occur when the Shen is weak. When Heart Qi is deficient palpitations, irregular heartbeat, and heart failure will occur.

How do we diagnose weak Qi? When looking at the tongue of a Qi-deficient animal, there will be little or no tone to the tongue. The tongue will appear weak, pale, wet, and floppy, often falling out of the mouth and drooping over the teeth and lips. The tongue may also be swollen due to the excess moisture present. Lack of energy, fatigue, and weakness may be present. Geriatric pets tend to have weaker Qi.

The good news is that Qi can be boosted by feeding Qi tonic foods. Feeding a healthy, species-appropriate diet will support good digestion and conversion of the food into energy or Qi. All meats are Qi tonics, although some are stronger than others. A meat-based diet (which is species-appropriate for dogs and cats) should form the basis of the feeding protocol. Choose the meat source based on the energetics listed in the previous chapter. Pets that need cooling foods can be fed rabbit or duck as a meat source while pets that need warming foods might be fed lamb or chicken.

Some grains are also good Qi tonics, including millet, corn, oats, brown rice, and long grain white rice. Again, feed according to energetics: millet and brown rice are cooling while oats and white rice are warming and corn is neutral. Vegetables, fruits, and nuts that are good Qi tonics include pumpkin, squash, sweet potatoes, yams, figs, chestnuts, lychee, lotus seed, and Shiitake mushrooms.

There is a lot of truth to the saying "like feeds like". I like to supplement the diet with whichever organ is suffering from deficiency. For animals with heart disease, feed heart; for animals with liver disease, feed liver; for animals with kidney disease, feed kidneys; for animals with lung disease, feed lungs. Animals with stomach or digestive deficiencies will benefit from being fed tripe, which is part of a cow's stomach. The tripe should be green tripe which still contains beneficial bacteria and digestive enzymes (and smells awful). Bleached white tripe smells better, but it has been cleaned and has lost most of the beneficial substances.

QI TONIC FOODS

MEATS: rabbit, beef, chicken, green tripe, lamb, goat, eel, carp, trout, herring, mackerel

GRAINS: millet, corn, oats, long-cook white rice, brown rice

VEGETABLES: pumpkin, squash, sweet potatoes, yams, figs, chestnuts, lychee, lotus seed, shiitake mushroom

FOODS TO DRAIN DAMP

MEATS: anchovy, mackerel, sardine

VEGETABLES: alfalfa, Adzuki beans, celery, kidney beans, Mung beans, mushrooms, radish, turnip, asparagus, kelp, lentil, lettuce, pumpkin

GRAINS: barley, corn, rye, soybean, buckwheat, Job's tears

HERBS: horseradish, marjoram, parsley, pepper

FRUITS: lemon, cranberry, papaya

FOODS TO WARM THE SPLEEN

MEATS: venison, lamb, kidney, shrimp, lobster

HERBS: chives, garlic, dill seed, fennel seed, cinnamon, cloves, nutmeg, ginger, basil, rosemary, thyme, cardamom

FRUITS: raspberries

Whenever your pet has a stomach upset, ginger will sooth and aid digestion because it warms the Spleen. Pets suffering from vomiting and/or diarrhea can be soothed by feeding a warm congee, which is made by mincing 1 cup chicken with 1 teaspoon grated ginger and 1 cup white or brown rice. Put in a large soup pot, fill with water, and cook slowly all day until all ingredients are dissolved. Congee can be refrigerated for up to four days and frozen for up to four months. It's a good idea to keep some on hand!

LORA LU'S QI TONIC STEW

- 5 to 6 pounds of skinless chicken (half white meat, half dark meat) – warming, Qi tonic

- ½ pound chicken liver – warming, Blood tonic

- 3 large sweet potatoes peeled and diced – neutral, Qi tonic

- 1 large turnip – cooling, drains Damp (keep Spleen happy)

- 1 acorn squash peeled and diced – warming, Qi tonic

- 1 butternut squash peeled and diced – warming, Qi tonic

- 1 cup brown rice – cooling, Qi tonic

- 2 cups chopped Shiitake mushrooms – cooling, Qi tonic

- 1 quart organic chicken stock and water to fill slow cooker

This recipe contains approximately 24% carbohydrates, 26% fat, and 50% protein. Each cup contains about 250 calories. Feed about 1 cup per 25 pounds body weight twice daily. Cook in slow cooker all day. If you use a whole cut up chicken, be sure to remove the bones after cooking. Share with your pet for an energizing meal that is energetically balanced!

Add probiotics, vitamin D3, and calcium or mineral supplement at the time of feeding. Fish oil capsules should be given to supplement vitamin E and Omega 3's. Currently, my preferred source of vitamin D3 and calcium/minerals is Rx Vitamins for Pets. I use AllerG-3 for my Omega 3 and vitamin E supplement. I use Rx Biotics or Synacore as my probiotic source. Dose according to label directions.

This diet is not meant to be served day after day for long periods of time. It should be rotated with other recipes, making sure to include a variety of ingredients. Eggs, leafy greens, liver and other organ meats, and different protein sources will afford a broader spectrum of nutrients.

BLOOD IS THE BASIS OF LIFE

Blood flows through the veins and arteries supplying oxygen, moisture, and nourishment to the organs to keep them functioning well. It keeps tendons, skin, and hair healthy, strong, and flexible. It lubricates joints and allows smooth movement. Blood nourishes the mind and is the material basis for mental activity. It ensures good sleep, keeps us calm, and ensures good memory. It provides sensation to the limbs, skin, and muscles and keeps us grounded. Blood provides moisture and lubrication to the eyes. Without good blood supply organs fail and the body dies.

We get blood from the food we eat. The Spleen transports and transforms food to make blood. What we eat affects the quality of our blood. Damp or cold foods will slow and inhibit the Spleen's ability to transform food into blood. Eating too little, too much, too fast, at irregular times, or poor quality foods will cause us to be blood deficient. Many vegan, vegetarian, and low fat diets lack blood building foods. Inflammatory bowel disease, colitis, intestinal parasites, and abnormal gut flora, with chronic mal-absorption of nutrients can result in blood deficiency.

Symptoms of blood deficiency include weak tendons that are easily injured, hind end weakness, and ruptured cruciate ligaments. There will be less lubrication of the joints and less joint fluid, resulting in deterioration of the joint cartilage covering the ends of the bones, leading to arthritis. Blood deficiency can be seen as a loss of pigment from the nose, hair or paw pads. The hair will be dry and brittle with excessive shedding. Small dry flakes can be seen throughout the coat and the pet may scratch a lot. Nails may be dry and brittle and will break easily. The tongue will be pale pink and dry.

Sleeplessness, anxiety, confusion, and loss of memory will occur. Animals may be easily frightened if they are blood deficient. There may be a loss of sensation to the limbs, skin, and muscles, resulting in numbness and tingling. Dry eyes, decreased tear production, and weak vision may occur. Anemia may or may not be noted when blood is tested at the laboratory, but blood deficiency can be diagnosed even with blood parameters in the normal range.

Treatment for blood deficiency includes the use of Blood Tonic foods. These foods are generally rich in iron, B vitamins, and amino acids. Rich, red meats like beef, liver, and heart are good blood tonics. Whole eggs and sardines are also great additions to the diet. Carrots, kidney beans, and parsley are blood tonic vegetables. Parsley has the added bonus of freshening the breath. Dates and apricots offer a sweet treat rich in blood building nutrients. Foods that are not specifically listed as blood tonics, but may also be helpful, include anything orange or red, like sweet potatoes, yams, beets, and pumpkin. Dark leafy greens like spinach, kale, and kelp are also great additions to a blood tonic meal.

Once the blood is re-enforced, the blood also has to move. Blood is moved by Qi, so Qi tonic foods must also be added to the recipe. Avoid foods that are cold and damp so the Spleen can function well to transform food into blood. Avoid dairy products, refined grains, sugars, carbohydrates, and cold (temperature at feeding) foods. Do not feed ice cubes as treats. Refer back to the previous chapter to find foods to warm the Spleen and drain the Damp.

BLOOD TONIC FOODS

MEATS: sardines, whole eggs, beef, liver, heart, bone marrow, pork, oysters

VEGETABLES: parsley, carrots, kidney beans, aduki beans, spinach, watercress, alfalfa sprouts

GRAINS & SEEDS: barley, corn, oats, sweet rice, wheat bran, black sesame

FRUITS: apricots, dates, longan

OTHER FOODS THAT MAY HELP BUILD BLOOD

MEATS: dark meat chicken, tuna, swordfish

GRAINS, SEEDS, & NUTS: walnuts, quinoa, brown rice, lentils

VEGETABLES: kelp, sweet potatoes, yams, beets, pumpkin, kale, cabbage, chard, broccoli

CHILI DOG BLOOD TONIC STEW (grain free)

- 5 pounds beef cut up into small cubes – warming, Blood tonic

- 5 large organic carrots peeled and chopped – neutral, Blood tonic, moves blood

- 5 cloves fresh organic garlic peeled and crushed – warming, drains damp, transforms phlegm, moves blood, adds flavor!

- 1 bunch fresh organic parsley chopped – cooling, Blood tonic, moves blood

- 2 cans organic low salt kidney beans – neutral, Blood tonic

- 1 cup chopped organic Shiitake mushrooms – cooling, Qi tonic to move the blood

- Put all ingredients in a slow cooker. Add water to fill the pot. Cook all day.

This recipe contains approximately 20% carbohydrates, 27% fat, and 53% protein. Each cup contains approximate 375 calories. Feed about 3/4 cup per 25 pounds of body weight twice daily. Not all dogs digest kidney beans well. If you know your dog does not do well with beans, 1 cup of brown or wild rice would be a good substitute. Add probiotics, vitamin D3, and calcium or mineral supplement at the time of feeding. Fish oil capsules should be given to supplement vitamin E and Omega 3's. Currently, my preferred source of vitamin D3 and calcium/minerals is Rx Vitamins for Pets. I use AllerG-3 for my Omega 3 and vitamin E supplement. Dose according to label directions. Serve warm.

This diet is not meant to be served day after day for long periods of time. It should be rotated with other recipes, making sure to include a variety of ingredients. Eggs, leafy greens, liver and other organ meats, and different protein sources will afford a broader spectrum of nutrients.

HOW TO DRAIN PHLEGM

What is phlegm and why do we care about it? Phlegm is a thick sticky substance produced in the body. Examples include mucus from the nose, thick discharges from the eyes or ears, vaginal discharges, thick secretions from cysts, and a sticky substance coating the tongue. Phlegm is formed when heat is present and moisture is lost, for example during illness when a fever is present. The heat from the body cooks the body fluids and causes them to accumulate and congeal. (Think of a pot of stew simmering on the stove all day – it thickens as it cooks and moisture evaporates.) Respiratory infections with fever can result in thick discharges from the nose and possibly thick mucus in the chest. Cough and chronic asthma can both be related to phlegm.

Pets that are fed a lifetime diet of dry food are eating a heat-processed, low moisture food, which is high in carbohydrates and will eventually lead to increased phlegm production in the body. People who have diets high in refined sugars and fried foods will also develop phlegm problems, notably obesity, as body fat is a form of phlegm. Dairy products like cheese, milk, and ice cream are actually a form of phlegm produced by animals. Diets high in dairy products will lead to increased phlegm in the body. These types of diets lead to excess dampness which damages the Spleen and decreases its ability to transform and transport nutrients, which causes phlegm to be produced.

Phlegm can also occur when there is excess cold in the body. Excess cold slows the movement of Qi and results in "freezing" of the liquids in the body like ice cubes being made from water. The smooth flow of Qi will keep the fluids moving. With excess cold, the liquids in the body stop moving, become stagnant, and transform into phlegm. Feeding cold foods to your pets can have the same effect. So when you take a meal out of the refrigerator or freezer, you must warm it to body temperature before feeding. This can be accomplished using the microwave, with gentle warming on the stove or in the oven, by adding hot water, or by placing the container holding the meal into a bowl of hot water.

Phlegm can also occur when there is excess wind, drying the fluids and making them thicker. Yes, your mother was right when she told you not to go out with wet hair on a cold, windy day because you would catch a cold. The cold and wind freeze and dry the fluids in the body, leading to mucus, or phlegm, production. Allergies are considered a wind and heat condition, so the thick nasal and eye discharge are forms of phlegm caused by the wind and heat.

Excess phlegm can manifest itself in the body in many ways. One of the most common in pets is "dry eye" or KCS, where there is not enough tear production. Instead of making liquid, moisturizing tears, the eyes produce a thick, sticky mucous to help protect the corneas. It doesn't work very well because many animals eventually go blind from the chronic irritation suffered by the eyes.

Thick nasal secretions causing a stuffy nose, thick, waxy ear discharges, and sticky phlegm stuck on the middle of the tongue are symptoms of phlegm in the body. Phlegm can also manifest as nodules or tumors, both benign and malignant.

Treatment of phlegm requires dilution of the phlegm by adding moisture; Qi tonics must also be added to move the moisture through the body. The phlegm needs to be softened by warming. A warm soup can get things moving by adding liquid and warmth. Yep, mom was right again when she made a big pot of chicken soup when you were sick from going outside in the wind and cold. The congee mentioned in a previous chapter is a good example of a warming soup. The phlegm needs to be transformed with increased moisture and energy. Blood tonics will add moisture because blood is the liquid of the body. Foods that soften and transform the phlegm will help it dissolve and move through the body.

Foods that transform phlegm include almonds, clams, apples, pears, oranges, ginger, lemon or grapefruit peels, garlic, peppermint, pepper, radish, kelp or seaweed, and thyme. Small amounts of a few of these ingredients can be added to meals to help dissolve phlegm.

To transform phlegm you must eliminate dry food from the diet. Add moisture to the food. Feed food at body temperature or a bit warmer. Feed diets that are easy to digest so the Spleen doesn't have to work so hard. Slow-cooked meals are already partially digested and make the work of the Spleen very easy. Feed diets that are low in carbohydrates and refined sugars. Avoid dairy products. Feed Qi tonics to get the phlegm moving. Phlegm that sits in one place too long can become a tumor later in life. We have to increase the moisture, but we also have to make it move.

FOODS TO TRANSFORM PHLEGM
MEATS: clams, crab, lobster, shrimp, prawn
HERBS: garlic, ginger, pepper, peppermint, thyme, basil, fennel, rosemary, caraway, cardamom, marjoram
VEGETABLES: pepper, radish, kelp or seaweed, water chestnut, olive, Shiitake mushroom
NUTS: almonds, walnuts
FRUITS: apples, lemon or grapefruit peel, orange, pear

Add Qi tonics as indicated in the chapter on Qi.

TRANSFORMATION RATION

- 1 whole chicken, cut up, skin removed – Qi tonic, warming

- 3 apples – transform phlegm, cooling

- 1 cup barley – draining, blood tonic, cooling

- 2 sweet potatoes – Qi tonic, neutral

- 3 stalks celery – cooling, draining

Place in slow cooker, add water, and cook all day. Remove bones from chicken and break apart chicken until shredded. This recipe contains about 300 calories per cup, with 33% carbohydrates, 23% fat, and 44% protein. Serve about 1 cup per 25 pounds body weight twice daily. Oats, which are warming and a Qi tonic, could be used instead of barley if pet is cold and needs warming. Add probiotics, vitamin D3, and calcium or mineral supplement at the time of feeding. Fish oil capsules should be given to supplement vitamin E and Omega 3's. Currently, my preferred source of vitamin D3 and calcium/minerals is Rx Vitamins for Pets. I use AllerG-3 for my Omega 3 and vitamin E supplement. Dose according to label directions. Serve warm.

This diet is not meant to be served day after day for long periods of time. It should be rotated with other recipes, making sure to include a variety of ingredients. Eggs, leafy greens, liver and other organ meats, and different protein sources will afford a broader spectrum of nutrients.

STAGNATION

The definition of stagnation is "having stopped, to cease to run or flow". Qi or blood can become stagnant, not moving freely throughout the body. When blood becomes stagnant, it causes pain and swelling at the site where the blood pools. Without Qi, blood cannot move. Once blood and Qi stop moving, stagnation occurs.

There are many causes of Qi or blood stagnation. It can occur secondary to frustration. In pets frustration can be caused by confinement, excess competition in the pack, lack of exercise, or lack of human interaction. Qi or blood stagnation can be caused by excess cold, so food should always be fed at room temperature. Yang deficiency, which is too much cold and not enough warmth in the body, can also cause stagnation.

Qi or blood stagnation can be caused by excess phlegm obstructing the movement of Qi and blood. However, stagnation can also be the cause of phlegm. Stagnation can be caused by spinal misalignment, resulting in muscle spasms and decreased Qi and blood flow to the organs and muscles. Qi or blood stagnation can be caused by accidents or trauma causing bruising and pooling of blood.

Examples of stagnation include lumps, bumps, tumors, constipation, and bladder stones. Pain in the abdomen can be a sign of stagnation. Liver blood stagnation is one of the more common types of stagnation. Stagnation in the digestive tract can lead to a feeling of fullness and a loss of appetite. Pain in the joints from arthritis is also a form of stagnation. Stagnation is usually the source of pain. Animals suffering from stagnation may dislike being rubbed or massaged.

Symptoms of stagnation will include a purple or lavender tongue, but it could also be dark or deep red. (Think of the color of a bruise.) The location of the lavender color on the tongue will give information on the location of the stagnation in the body.

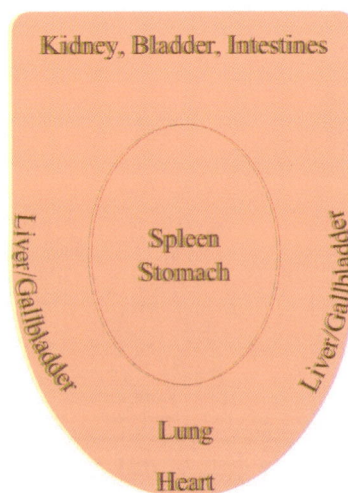

Diagnostic areas of the tongue

Frustration, anger, aggression, hyperactivity, irritability, and emotional outbursts are commonly seen when stagnation is present. Lethargy and inability to move may be a problem due to the deficiency of Qi (energy). Pets may seek warmth if the stagnation is due to a Yang and Qi deficiency. Warmth applied to an area of stagnation will help move the blood and decrease pain.

Treatment of stagnation includes feeding Qi tonics to get the stagnation to move. Many meats are Qi tonics, but chicken, crab, lamb, shrimp and venison are the best Qi tonics for moving stagnation. Most of the meats used to resolve stagnation are warming; this is because stagnation usually involves a Qi and Yang deficiency. Crab is the only cold meat that will move stagnation when heat is a problem. This could make for some expensive meals, so herbs may be a better selection to add to the diet in the case of stagnation with heat. Pumpkin is a great Qi tonic and will help get things moving. Other vegetables that resolve stagnation include carrots, parsley, radish, watercress, and garlic. Herbs, including coriander, ginger, turmeric, dill seed, and cloves move stagnation. Vinegar and orange or tangerine peels are also good for resolving stagnation.

Avoid foods that cause cold and damp and damage the Spleen, leading to stagnation. Avoid dairy products, refined sugars and carbohydrates, dry pet food, and cold foods.

FOODS TO RESOLVE STAGNATION

MEATS: chicken, crab, lamb, shrimp, venison

VEGETABLES: carrots, radish, watercress

HERBS: parsley, garlic, hawthorn berry, chive, clove, coriander, dill seed, garlic, ginger, turmeric, vinegar

FRUITS: orange or tangerine peel

START MY ENGINE STEW TO RESOLVE STAGNATION

- 3 pounds ground chicken or venison – Qi tonics, resolve stagnation, warming

- 6 medium sized carrots – Blood tonic, resolve stagnation, neutral

- 3 cups spinach – Blood tonic, cooling

- 1 cup parsley – Blood tonic, resolve stagnation, cooling

- 2 tablespoons grated fresh ginger root – resolve stagnation, warming

- 2 cups barley – Blood tonic, draining, cooling

Place in slow cooker and add water. Cook all day. The fat content of chicken will be higher than using venison (32% vs. 26%). If your pet needs a lower fat, chicken version, use whole chicken dark and white meat with the skin removed, which will lower the fat to 17%. Using ground chicken in the recipe will give approximately 34% carbohydrates, 32% fat, and 34% protein. Venison recipe will be approximately 35% carbohydrates, 26% fat, and 39% protein. Each cup contains approximately 200 calories. One cup per 20 pounds of body weight twice daily is a good starting point. Add probiotics, vitamin D3, and calcium or mineral supplement at the time of feeding. Fish oil capsules should be given to supplement vitamin E and Omega 3's. Currently, my preferred source of vitamin D3 and calcium/minerals is Rx Vitamins for Pets. I use AllerG-3 for my Omega 3 and vitamin E supplement. Dose according to label directions.

This diet is not meant to be served day after day for long periods of time. It should be rotated with other recipes, making sure to include a variety of ingredients. Eggs, leafy greens, liver and other organ meats, and different protein sources will afford a broader spectrum of nutrients.

TREATING PETS WITH CANCER

When dealing with cancer patients, feeding real food is probably more important than any other time in your pet's life. You are fighting to save a life. Fresh fruits and vegetables should be organic, meats should be pasture-raised instead of raised in feedlots, and grains need to be non-GMO and organic. Pets with cancer should never be fed processed dry foods, as those foods will contribute to dampness, phlegm, and stagnation, which are all problems in cancer patients. Semi-moist foods should never be fed to any animal because they are filled with dyes, sugars, and harmful preservatives, not to mention being made with horrendous ingredients. You might be able to get away with a very high quality canned food if you can find one without added glutens or binders. Home cooked diets or raw foods will be your best options to treat patients with cancer because you can control the ingredients. Pets undergoing chemotherapy or radiation will probably be barred from raw food diets by the oncologist treating the pet. Treats for pets with cancer must be given the same consideration; make sure they are made with only the highest quality, organic ingredients, or make them yourself.

What is cancer? Cancer is a disorder of cell growth where abnormal cells grow unchecked by the body. Abnormal cells are always forming in the body, but a healthy immune system will attack and eliminate those abnormal cells because they are recognized as being foreign to the body. Sometimes large masses or tumors are formed which may be easier to diagnose than infiltrative forms of cancer. Lymphoma or lymphosarcoma of the bowel is a type of cancer that is commonly infiltrative and more difficult to diagnose. Invasive cancers that are not removable require therapies other than surgery for treatment. Chemotherapy, food therapy, and herbal therapy can be invaluable here.

What causes cancer? Cancer can be caused by external toxins or by internal disorders. Emotional stress opens the body to more mutations by cells and inability to kill those cells. Poor diets loaded with toxins will lead to dampness, phlegm, stagnation, and the growth of nodules or tumors. Disorders of the immune system caused by being constantly bombarded with vaccines, drugs, environmental radiation, and pollution will leave the body vulnerable to an attack by cancerous cells.

An imbalance in the flow of Qi or a blockage of the flow of Qi allows an accumulation of dampness. Dampness damages the Spleen and decreases its ability to transport and transform nutrients to support the body. Stagnation occurs, and a tumor will start to form. The Spleen can be overwhelmed by poor nutrition, resulting in poor nutrient usage, fatigue, and muscle wasting. Animals may have sudden and severe weight loss, but the owners may not notice. A ten pound cat that loses one pound has lost ten percent of his body weight!

Blood Deficiency can also be a cause of cancer in patients. Blood deficiency will occur in patients chronically fed poor diets or exposed to environmental toxins like cigarette smoke or pollution. These patients are chronically dry, with flaky dry coats and dry noses and foot pads. Excessive use of drugs, vaccines, and stress to the immune system will cause a blood deficiency.

Symptoms of cancer can be anything. Fatigue, muscle weakness, increased sleeping, increased or decreased thirst, hunger, or urination can occur. Pets with stomach or intestinal cancers can actually have increased hunger because they are not absorbing the nutrients they are eating. Some pets will eat dirt, seeking minerals that they are missing from their food. Weight loss will occur unless the patient has a tumor so large it is adding body weight. Tumors of the spleen or liver can grow to the size of a basketball. Eventually the pet will stop eating and severe muscle wasting will occur.

The tongue in pets with cancer can be purple, with or without a phlegm coating, due to blood stagnation; or they can be dark, brick red due to heat and inflammation in the body. Dogs with severe blood deficiency cancer will have a pale, dry tongue. Excessive panting is usually seen in pets with cancer due to Yin deficiency or pain due to stagnation.

All the herbs, vitamins, and therapies in the world are not as important as nutrition when fighting cancer. If a pet is undergoing surgery, followed by radiation and chemotherapy, the cancer may be cured, but the pet will still die if it doesn't eat. Feeding a poor quality diet will not allow the body to return to good health.

All the therapies in the world are not as important as the ability to *live* while treating the cancer. Be sure to focus on happiness of the patient instead of constantly dragging the pet to more and more specialists. Take time every day to do something your pet enjoys; massage, a walk in the park, lying in the yard in the sun, whatever makes your pet happy.

Cancer cells grow by utilizing sugars. They don't utilize proteins and fats as well as carbohydrates. So most of the calories in the diet need to come from proteins and fats, along with healthy carbohydrates like fresh vegetables, not processed, refined products. It is preferable to feed foods with a low glycemic index. The glycemic index measures how quickly a food can raise blood sugar levels. Glucose, or sugar, has a glycemic index of 100. White potatoes have a higher glycemic index than sugar. All dry dog foods are high in carbohydrates, so they should not be used for pets with cancer.

Look for whole grains with low glycemic values. Whole grains are a good source of fiber, B vitamins, calcium, iron, and trace minerals. Barley is a blood tonic grain which is also cooling (Yin tonic) and draining (drains damp), so it would be perfectly suitable in a meal prepared for a pet with cancer. Other low glycemic foods include pumpkin, sweet potatoes, winter squash, tomatoes, and whole wheat pasta. Pumpkin and sweet potatoes are also blood tonics.

Cooked cruciferous vegetables like purple cabbage, broccoli, cabbage, cauliflower, kale, and Brussels sprouts are nutritious additives that are good for fighting cancer. Up to 25% of the meal can be made up of dark, leafy greens if there is excessive heat in the body (dark red tongue, panting). The dark leafy greens also support the liver and help the liver process toxins, especially if the pet is undergoing chemotherapy. Olive oil or flax seed oil may be used to add some fat calories to the diet and they may be better tolerated than fish oils, which may cause diarrhea, when excess heat is present.

Meats are good Qi tonics, so meat should form the basis of the diet. Qi is needed to move the stagnation. Red meats can be a bit more stagnating than other meats. Rabbit would be a great cooling food that is a strong Qi tonic. Gizzards, white fish, oily fish like salmon and sardines, chicken, and turkey would also be good meat choices. Organ meats like liver and hearts can add amino acids and vitamins not found in muscle meats. Eggs are great blood tonics for these pets. Look for organic, cage-free eggs from chickens that were fed non-GMO feed and no antibiotics.

Herbs can be used to resolve stagnation and phlegm and to drain damp. Hawthorn, citrus peel, turmeric, coriander, garlic, vinegar, and ginger will get the Qi moving. Garlic needs to be freshly peeled and crushed in order to get the best benefits.

For blood deficient cancers, blood tonics need to be added. These are the pets with the pale, dry tongues and dry, flaky skin. Beef, tuna, liver, sardines, and eggs, can be mixed with dark, leafy green vegetables, beets, aduki beans, organ meats, figs, dates, apricots, blueberries, or raspberries as blood tonics.

The kidneys need to be fortified when pets are being treated for cancer. The kidneys like "baby" foods, like alfalfa sprouts and barley sprouts. Seeds and nuts are also "baby" foods, so black sesame seeds, sesame butter, or almond butter would be good to use. Kelp, clams, and sardines, which originate from the sea and are salty, make the kidneys happy. Root vegetables like parsnips, turnips, carrots, radishes, and sweet potatoes tonify the kidneys while helping drain toxins and drain damp. Asparagus is also good for draining damp.

Foods that will transform phlegm are important for treating cancer. Apples, pears, walnuts, or almonds can be used as treats or incorporated into a meal. Kelp or seaweed is also great for transforming phlegm.

Avoid foods that cause cold and damp in the Spleen. Avoid dry pet foods, dairy products, refined sugars, and cold (temperature and energetic) foods. Keep the bowel healthy with good intestinal flora. Add a high quality probiotic to the diet. Seventy to 85% of the immune system lives in the bowel and the immune system needs to fight the cancer. Digestive enzymes may make the work of digestion easier and would be great to add if your pet will eat them readily.

Medicating pets with cancer can be difficult. Many of these patients will need multiple medications multiple times a day. Hiding medications in food can contribute to food aversion. Food aversion can be the biggest challenge faced when treating pets with cancer. Food rotation is extremely important so the pet will not develop food aversion. If you are having trouble getting the pet to eat, do not over-feed a food when they like something. If they feel nauseous after eating, they will avoid that food in the future. Do not make large batches of food if your pet has food aversion, unless you plan to eat the stew yourself!

Small amounts of garlic, parmesan cheese, tomato sauce (with no sugar!), fish sautéed in a little butter, or ground cinnamon on top of the food may stimulate the appetite. Sometimes separating the proteins from the carbohydrates will help, as well. Feed small amounts often, up to five or six times daily. Try to make the diet as well-balanced as possible, given the constraints of what the pet will eat. If the only thing the pet will eat is a piece of dry kibble or a spoonful of yogurt, feed those, even though they are not on the "good" list.

LIFELINE LOAF FOR A PET WITH CANCER

- 2 pounds ground chicken or lean beef – warm, Qi tonic, Resolves stagnation

- 1/2 pound chicken livers – warm, Blood tonic

- 4 eggs – neutral, Blood tonic, Yin tonic

- 3 grated carrots – neutral, Blood tonic, Resolves stagnation

- 1 cup chopped spinach – cool, Blood tonic, Yin tonic

- 1 grated apple – cool, Transform phlegm

- 1 cup chopped Shiitake mushrooms – cool, Qi tonic, Drain damp

- 2 cloves crushed garlic – warm, Yang tonic, Drains damp, Transform Phlegm, Resolve stagnation

- 1 cup pumpkin – warm, Qi tonic

Mix all ingredients together and fill large baking pan. Bake in the oven at 325 degrees for 1 hour. Each cup contains approximately 275 calories. Feeding one cup per 25 pounds of body weight twice daily is a good starting point. Using chicken, the diet will contain approximately 13% carbohydrates, 45% fat, and 42% protein. With 95% lean beef, the proportions will be closer to 15% carbohydrates, 35% fat, and 50% protein.

Add probiotics, vitamin D3, and calcium or mineral supplement at the time of feeding. Fish oil capsules should be given to supplement vitamin E and Omega 3's. Currently, my preferred source of vitamin D3 and calcium/minerals is Rx Vitamins for Pets. I use AllerG-3 for my Omega 3 and vitamin E supplement. Dose according to label directions.

This diet is not meant to be served day after day for long periods of time. It should be rotated with other recipes, making sure to include a variety of ingredients.

YOU ARE WHAT YOU EAT

by "Mom"

It's a simple concept really, but it holds true. With the help and guidance of Dr. Judy and her pet food webinars I became energized to learn how to safely home cook for Dexter and to use the principals of Chinese Medicine food therapies to address his medical condition.

The quality of food is vital and also affects the energetics. When at all possible, I choose organic and fresh foods. If I cannot find organic, I look for non-GMO, hormone-free, antibiotic-free, grass-fed, and humanely raised. I do sometimes cut up organic fruits and vegetables and place them in the freezer until I cook a recipe, but it always goes in the freezer fresh.

Balance is the key word when I'm preparing Dexter's meals. Just because he may be "hot" during the summer, I do not want to feed him all cooling or cold foods. I want the food energetics to be on the cool to neutral side. In the winter I shoot for warm to neutral. Then I want to go back and add in foods that help drain his damp, move his Qi, and resolve stagnation.

Switching Dexter from a dry kibble to home cooked meals should have been done gradually and taken a couple of weeks. But I went all out and did a full switch. Poor Dexter paid the price with an upset belly and a quick trip to the veterinarian's office. Once his belly got back on track, we gradually switched to our home cooked meals.

Important Feeding/Cooking Guidelines:

•Meals should be brought up to body temperature before consuming. I personally do this by adding hot water from our water dispenser. I ensure the temperature is correct by placing my finger inside the mixture. You could also warm the bowl or warm the meal in a plastic bag in a bowl of warm water.

•You will need to add the appropriate vitamins, minerals, and supplements to each meal. Probiotics cannot be added to hot food, or they lose their viability.

•Always speak with your veterinarian before switching your dog over to a home cooked diet. If your veterinarian is not comfortable in guiding you on your journey, please contact a Certified Veterinary Food Therapist through The Chi Institute of Traditional Chinese Veterinary Medicine.

•Feed your dog 2 to 4 times a day, depending on your schedule and their dietary needs.

•A typical dog should get about 20 to 30 calories per pound, depending on their health and activity level. Dexter weighs 28 lbs and eats about 600 calories a day depending on his activities and health.

•Meat and protein calories are typically between 50-60% of the overall calories per day. Organ meats consist of approximately 30% of these calories. Liver should not be given in large amounts daily, but 2-3 times a week is usually okay.

•I typically switch up Dexter's meals every week. If your dog has a sensitive stomach, you may want to do this on a more gradual scale.

•I wash all my fruits and vegetables and typically remove the skins, seeds, and pits prior to cooking.

•The majority of Dexter's meals are cooked in a slow cooker on low for about 8 to 10 hours.

•Each recipe I use has approximately 500 calories. You can edit the quantity according to your dog's size and dietary needs.

•These are just general guidelines; once again, please speak with your veterinarian to address your dog's needs.

Food Prep and Tips:

•**Meats**-Trim off excess fat and gristle and discard. Cut the meat across the grain into thin, uniform strips about 1-inch-square so that all the pieces cook evenly. (It's easiest to do this if the meat is partially frozen).

•**Substitutions**–Tongue is the organ of the heart and may be substituted if you are unable to find heart.

•**Fish**-Start with a good filet knife and flat surface such as a cutting board. Filet the fish, removing bones, innards, head and tail. This can be done at most fish markets when you purchase the fish.

•**Fruits and Vegetables**-Under running water, wash fruits and vegetables with a produce brush to remove dirt and surface bacteria. Peel or remove skin, seeds and cores. Cut into 1-inch chunks.

•**Pumpkins and Squash** preparation can be challenging. Option 1: Start by using a saw to cut the top off. Remove the seeds and pulp. Place pumpkin on a baking sheet in a 350 degree Fahrenheit oven for 45 minutes, or until pumpkin is tender. Option 2: Start by using a saw to cut the top off. Remove the seeds and pulp. Cut into 1" chunks for slow cooker recipes. Option 3: Purchase organic pre-cut or chunks in a can!

•**Drop Cookies**-Line a cookie sheet with parchment paper. Drop tablespoons of the mixture on to the prepared baking sheet leaving 1 inch between each cookie.

•**Dehydrating**-Dry meat between 145 to155 degrees Fahrenheit for a minimum of 6 to12 hours. Slice meat into 1-inch by 2-inch strips ¼-inch thick. Once the meat is sufficiently dry, take out the strips and place them on a clean surface. With a paper towel, pat off excess oil and allow meat to cool. To check to see if the meat is done, attempt to bend it in half. If it bends and does not crack, it needs more time. If it breaks in half it's just right.

•Fruits and vegetables can be dried by cooking at 145 to 155 degrees Fahrenheit for 4 to 12 hours. Remove all the skin and seeds from the fruits and vegetables. Cut into 1-inch by 2-inch strips ¼-inch thick. Once the fruits and vegetables are sufficiently dry, take out the strips and place them on a clean surface. With a paper towel, pat off excess oil and allow the vegetables to cool. To check to see if they are done, attempt to bend one in half. If it bends and doesn't crack, it needs more time. If it breaks in half it's just right.

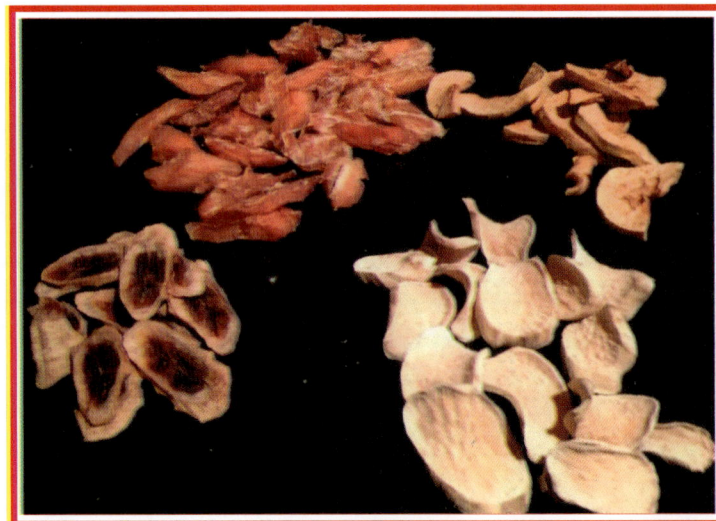

JUST THE SLOW COOKER

I love making my meals in the slow cooker whenever possible. It's a pretty easy way to cook healthy meals that I don't have to think too hard about. For these recipes, after your fruits and vegetables are cleaned, cut, de-seeded and peeled, and the meat is cubed, all you have to do is place in the slow cooker, cover with water, put the lid on, set it on low heat and wait 8 to 12 hours! Voila! It's that easy.

To serve you can either drain the juices out, or leave them in. Dogs need moisture, so I typically ladle out the food portion and add a few ladles of the broth to each meal. When using a slow-cooker recipe, you can make enough food for quite a few days.

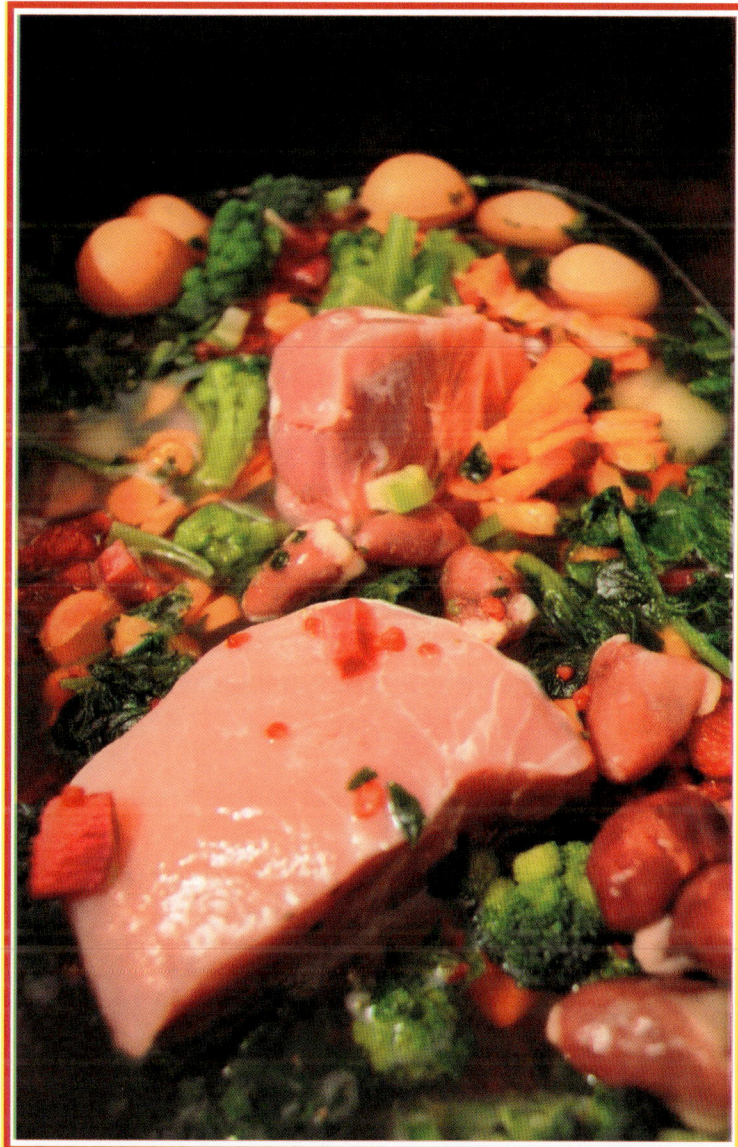

Alligator Chowder

This is a tasty, neutral to cool meal. Loaded with Blood and Qi tonics; good for draining damp. Perfect for a summer day.

- •3 ounces Alligator Meat-Cool
- •3.5 ounces Beef Liver-Neutral, Blood tonic
- •2 ounces Sweet Potatoes-Neutral, Qi tonic
- •2 ounces Celery-Cool, drains damp
- •1 ounce Carrots-Neutral, Blood tonic, resolve stagnation
- •1/8 cup dry Pearled Barley-Cool, Blood tonic, Yin tonic, drains damp
- •2 Sprigs Parsley-Neutral, Blood tonic, resolves stagnation

1)Clean all the vegetables. Peel the carrots and sweet potatoes. Cut into 4" chunks.
2)Cut the alligator and beef into 1" chunks.
3)Place the alligator, beef, sweet potatoes, celery, barley, and parsley into the slow cooker. Fill the slow cooker with water to cover the food.
4)Place the lid onto the pot, put on low, and simmer for 8-10 hours. You will want to ensure your meat is fully cooked.
5)Strain out the water; place the meal in a container or bowl.
500 Calories, Fat 12%, Protein 52%

Hawaiian Style Yellowfin Tuna

A nice neutral meal that builds blood and keeps it flowing.
Perfect for any day.

- 6.75 ounces Yellowfin Tuna-Neutral, Blood tonic, drains damp
- 2.25 ounces Beef Liver-Neutral, Blood tonic
- 2 ounces Pineapple Chunks-Neutral, transforms phlegm
- 1 ounce Tomato-Cool, Yin tonic
- ¼ cup dry Pearled Barley-Cool, Yin tonic, Blood tonic, drains damp

1)Clean the tomatoes, cut into bite sized chunks.
2)Cut the tuna and beef into 1" chunks.
3)Place the tuna, beef, pineapple, barley, and tomatoes into the slow cooker. Fill the slow cooker with water to cover the food.
4)Place the lid onto the pot, put on low, and simmer for 8-10 hours. You will want to ensure your meat is fully cooked.
5)Strain out the water; place the meal in a container or bowl. Dinner is served!
504 Calories, Fat 9%, Protein 53%

Taco Friday!

A nice neutral meal good for any Friday night party!
Nice Blood tonics and good for draining damp.

- 7 ounces Ground Beef, 95% Lean-Neutral, Blood tonic, Qi tonic
- 3.5 ounces Beef Liver-Neutral, Blood tonic
- 1 ounce Tomato-Cool, Yin tonic
- 1 ounce Lettuce-Cool, drains damp
- 1/8 cup dry Sweet Jasmine Rice-Neutral, Yang tonic, Qi tonic

1)Clean the tomatoes and lettuce, cut into bite-sized chunks.
2)Cut the beef liver into 1" chunks.
3)Place the beef liver, tomatoes, rice, and lettuce into the slow cooker. Crumble the ground hamburger into the slow cooker. Fill the slow cooker with water to cover the food.
4)Place the lid onto the pot, put on low and simmer for 8-10 hours. You will want to ensure your meat is fully cooked.
5)Strain out the water; place the meal in a container or bowl. It's taco Friday!
498 Calories, Fat 25%, Protein 55%

Wild About Cod

A refreshing meal for a hot summer day.

- •10.5 ounces Wild Caught Alaskan Cod-Cool, Yin tonic
- •3 ounces Beef Liver-Neutral, Blood tonic
- •3 ounces Sweet Potatoes-Neutral, Qi tonic
- •1 ounce Tomato-Cool, Yin tonic
- •1/8 cup dry Wild Rice-Cool, Qi tonic, Blood tonic

1)Clean the tomatoes and sweet potatoes. Cut the tomatoes into bite-sized chunks; do the same with the sweet potatoes after peeling them.
2)Cut the beef liver into 1" chunks.
3)Place the beef liver, cod, tomatoes, rice, and sweet potatoes into the slow cooker. Fill the slow cooker with water to cover the food.
4)Place the lid onto the pot, put on low, and simmer for 8-10 hours. You will want to ensure your meat is fully cooked.
5)Strain out the water; place the meal in a container or bowl. Now you are ready for a day at the beach!
504 Calories, Fat 10%, Protein 62%

Summer Feast

A refreshing meal for a hot summer day.

- •10.5 ounces Wild Caught Alaskan Cod-Cool, Yin tonic
- •3 ounces Chicken Liver-Warm, Blood tonic
- •3 ounces Sweet Potatoes-Neutral, Qi tonic
- •2 ounces Watermelon-Cool, drains damp
- •½ Pear-Cool, Yin tonic, transform phlegm
- •½ Apple-Neutral, Yin tonic, transform phlegm

1)Wash the fruits and sweet potatoes. Peel the pear, apple, and sweet potatoes. Cut the meat portion out of the watermelon and take out the seeds. Cut all the fruit and sweet potatoes into bite-sized chunks.
2)Cut the chicken liver and cod into 1" chunks.
3)Place all the ingredients into the slow cooker. Fill the slow cooker with water to cover the food.
4)Place the lid onto the pot, put on low, and simmer for 8-10 hours. You will want to ensure your meat is fully cooked.
5)Strain out the water; place the meal in a container or bowl. Now you are ready for hot summer day!
495 Calories, Fat 11%, Protein 56%

Beef It Up Buffalo Stew

A nice neutral meal to build blood and keep it flowing.

- 5 ounces Ground Beef, 95% Lean-Neutral, Blood tonic, Qi tonic
- 2 ounces ground Buffalo-Neutral, Qi tonic, Blood tonic
- 2.5 ounces Beef Liver-Neutral, Blood tonic
- 2 ounces Carrots-Neutral, Blood tonic, resolves stagnation
- 2 ounces Sweet Potatoes-Neutral, Qi tonic
- 1 ounce Celery-Cool, drains damp
- 1 ounce Tomato-Cool, Yin tonic
- 1 ounce Broccoli-Cool
- 1/8 cup dry Wild Rice-Cool, Qi tonic, Blood tonic

1)Clean the carrots, celery, tomatoes, broccoli, and sweet potatoes. Peel the carrots and sweet potatoes.
Cut all vegetables into bite-sized chunks.
2)Cut the beef liver into 1" chunks.
3)Place all the ingredients into the slow cooker and crumble the ground buffalo and beef on top. Fill
the slow cooker with water to cover the food.
4)Place the lid onto the pot, put on low, and simmer for 8-10 hours. You will want to ensure your meat
is fully cooked.
5)Strain out the water; place the meal in a container or bowl. A delightful dish for any day!
511 Calories, Fat 30%, Protein 44%

Beef & Scallops

A great cooling meal that helps drain the excess damp.

- •9 ounces Sea Scallops-Cool, Yin tonic
- •3 ounces Beef Liver-Neutral, Blood tonic
- •2 ounces Carrots-Neutral, Blood tonic, resolves stagnation
- •1 ounce Broccoli-Cool
- •1 ounce Celery-Cool, drains damp
- •1 ounce Cucumber-Cool, drains damp
- •1 Apple-Neutral, Yin tonic, transforms phlegm
- •1/8 cup dry Pearled Barley-Cool, Yin tonic, Blood tonic, drains damp

1)Wash and peel the vegetables. Clean and core the apple. Cut them into bite-sized chunks.
2)Cut the beef liver into 1" chunks. Rinse the sea scallops in cool water.
3)Place all the ingredients into the slow cooker. Fill the slow cooker with water to cover the food.
4)Place the lid onto the pot, put on low, and simmer for 8-10 hours. You will want to ensure your meat is fully cooked.
5)Strain out the water; place the meal in a container or bowl. A tasty dish for a hot summer night!
503 Calories, Fat 10%, Protein 50%

Cod With Eggplant

A wonderfully cool meal that will help drain excess damp and move stagnation.

- 11 ounces Wild Caught Alaskan Cod-Cool
- 2.5 ounces Beef Liver-Neutral, Blood tonic
- 2 ounces Sweet Potatoes-Neutral, Qi tonic
- 1 ounce Eggplant-Cool
- 1 ounce Celery-Cool, drains damp
- 1 ounce Tomato-Cool, Yin tonic
- 1 once Broccoli-Cool
- 1/8 cup dry Pearled Barley-Cool, Yin tonic, Blood tonic, drains damp

1)Clean the vegetables. Peel the sweet potato and eggplant. Cut all the vegetables into bite-sized chunks.
2)Cut the beef liver and cod into 1" chunks.
3)Place all the ingredients into the slow cooker. Fill the slow cooker with water to cover the food.
4)Place the lid onto the pot, put on low, and simmer for 8-10 hours. You will want to ensure your meat is fully cooked.
5)Strain out the water; place the meal in a container or bowl. A nice refreshing meal!
503 Calories, Fat 9%, Protein 61%

Beef and Wild Rice Medley

A tasty, neutral meal, full of Qi and Blood tonics!

•4 ounces Beef Round-Eye Chunks-Neutral, Qi tonic, Blood tonic

•1.5 ounces Beef Liver-Neutral, Blood tonic

•1.5 ounces Chicken Liver-Warm, Blood tonic

•1.5 ounces Vegetables, Mixed-Neutral

•½ Apple-Neutral, Yin tonic, transforms phlegm

•1/8 cup dry Wild Rice-Cool, Qi tonic, Blood tonic

1)Clean the vegetables and apple. Peel and core the apple; cut into bite-sized chunks.
2)Cut all the meat into 1" chunks.
3)Place all the ingredients into the slow cooker. Fill the slow cooker with water to cover the food.
4)Place the lid onto the pot, put on low, and simmer for 8-10 hours. You will want to ensure your meat is fully cooked.
5)Strain out the water; place the meal in a container or bowl. A great meal to get the Qi moving!
499 Calories, Fat 20%, Protein 55%

Clamfection

A delightful cooling dish to aid in draining damp and moving stagnation.
Packed with Qi and Blood tonics for an extra boost.
This would be great for dogs with dry eyes.

- 12 ounces Clam Meat-Cool, Yin tonic, transforms phlegm
- 3 ounces Beef Liver-Neutral, Blood tonic
- 4.5 ounces Carrots-Neutral, Blood tonic, resolves stagnation
- 1/8 cup dry Pearled Barley-Cool, Yin tonic, drains damp

1) Wash and peel the carrots; cut into bite-sized pieces.
2) Rinse the clam meat in a strainer.
3) Cut the liver into 1" chunks.
4) Place all the ingredients into the slow cooker. Fill the slow cooker with water to cover the food.
5) Place the lid onto the pot, put on low, and simmer for 8-10 hours. You will want to ensure your meat is fully cooked.
6) Strain out the water; place the meal in a container or bowl. A great meal to drain excess damp, transform phlegm, and move stagnation. **499 Calories, Fat 13%, Protein 35%**

Fruity Summer Pork Chops

A delicate little dish packed full of goodness.
Perfect for hot summers or anytime.

- 4.5 ounces Pork Chops, Boneless-Neutral, Yin tonic
- 2.5 ounces Beef Liver-Neutral, Blood tonic
- 1 ounce Spinach-Cool, Blood tonic, Yin tonic
- 1 Shiitake Mushroom-Neutral, Qi tonic, drains damp
- 1 Pear-Cool, Yin tonic, transforms phlegm
- 1 ounce Cucumber-Cool, drains damp
- ½ Banana-Cool, Yin tonic

1) Wash and peel the fruits and vegetables; cut into bite-sized pieces.
2) Cut the liver and pork into 1" chunks.
3) Place all the ingredients into the slow cooker. Fill the slow cooker with water to cover the food.
4) Place the lid onto the pot, put on low, and simmer for 8-10 hours. You will want to ensure your meat is fully cooked.
5) Strain out the water; place the meal in a container or bowl. A sweet dish to tempt any palate.
501 Calories, Fat 22%, Protein 41%

Leftovers

Packed with flavor, this dish is filled with food to get that stagnation moving,
with a healthy dose of Qi and Blood tonics.

- 6 ounces Beef Round-Eye Chunks-Neutral, Blood tonic, Qi tonic
- 1.5 ounces Beef Liver-Neutral, Blood tonic
- 3 ounces Carrots-Neutral, Blood tonic, resolves stagnation
- 2 ounces Tomato-Cool, Yin tonic
- 1 Orange-Cool, transforms phlegm
- 1/8 cup dry Wild Rice-Cool, Qi tonic, Blood tonic

1) Wash and peel the fruits and vegetables; cut into bite-sized pieces.
2) Cut the liver and beef into 1" chunks.
3) Place all the ingredients into the slow cooker. Fill the slow cooker with water to cover the food.
4) Place the lid onto the pot, put on low, and simmer for 8-10 hours. You will want to ensure your meat is fully cooked.
5) Strain out the water; place the meal in a container or bowl. This power dish will build blood and energy!

504 Calories, Fat 19%, Protein 54%

Gatorama Stew

A pleasant dish perfect for a hot summer afternoon.

- 7 ounces Wild Caught Alaskan Cod-Cool, Yin tonic
- 2 ounces Alligator Meat-Cool, Yin tonic
- 1ounce Pork Kidney-Neutral, Yin tonic, Blood tonic
- 1 ounce Cucumber-Cool, drains damp
- 1 ounce Cauliflower-Neutral
- 1 ounce Tomato-Cool, Yin tonic
- 1 Egg, Chicken-Neutral, Yin tonic, Blood tonic
- ½ ounce Spinach-Cool, Blood tonic, Yin tonic
- 1/8 cup dry Wild Rice-Cool, Qi tonic, Blood tonic

1)Wash and peel the vegetables; cut into bite-sized pieces.
2)Cut the meat into 1" chunks.
3)Place all the ingredients into the slow cooker. Fill the slow cooker with water to cover the food.
4)Place the lid onto the pot, put on low, and simmer for 8-10 hours. You will want to ensure your meat is fully cooked.
5)Remove the egg and peel the shell. Cut the egg into pieces and place in a container or dish. Strain out the water; place the remaining ingredients into the same dish.
502 Calories, Fat 21%, Protein 51%

Apple Beef Stew

This mouthwatering dish is full of Qi and Blood tonics. This would be a great meal for dogs with heart problems.

- 6.5 ounces Beef Round-Eye Chunks-Neutral, Blood tonic, Qi tonic
- 1 ounce Beef Heart-Neutral, Blood tonic
- 1 Apple-Neutral, Yin tonic, transforms phlegm
- 1 ounce Cucumber-Cool, drains damp
- 1 ounce Tomato-Cool, Yin tonic
- 1/8 cup dry Pearled Barley-Cool, Yin tonic, Blood tonic, drains damp

1) Wash and peel the fruits and vegetables; cut into bite sized pieces.
2) Cut the heart and beef into 1" chunks.
3) Place all the ingredients into the slow cooker. Fill the slow cooker with water to cover the food.
4) Place the lid onto the pot, put on low, and simmer for 8-10 hours. You will want to ensure your meat is fully cooked.
5) Strain out the water; place the meal in a container or bowl. A simple delight to energize the Qi.
498 Calories, Fat 18%, Protein 51%

Strawberries & Clams

A wonderfully cool dish to help drain the damp and transform phlegm.

- •12 ounces Clam Meat-Cool, Yin tonic, transforms phlegm
- •4 ounces Pork Kidney-Neutral, Yin tonic, Blood tonic
- •4 ounces Strawberries-Neutral, Yang tonic
- •3 ounces Celery-Cool, drains damp
- •1 Shiitake Mushroom-Neutral, Qi tonic, drains damp
- •1/8 cup dry Brown Rice-Cool, Qi tonic, Blood tonic

1)Wash and peel the fruits and vegetables; cut into bite-sized pieces.
2)Cut the kidney into 1" chunks.
3)Rinse the clam meat in a strainer.
4)Place all the ingredients into the slow cooker. Fill the slow cooker with water to cover the food.
5)Place the lid onto the pot, put on low, and simmer for 8-10 hours. You will want to ensure your meat is fully cooked.
6)Strain out the water; place the meal in a container or bowl. A perfect summer dish.
499 Calories, Fat 17%, Protein 37%

Crab Delight

A light meal, perfect for a warm day.
Great for draining excess damp and getting things moving. Great meal for pets with cancer that have heat.

- 8 ounces Crab Meat-Cool, resolves stagnation
- 3 ounces Beef Heart-Neutral, Blood tonic
- 1 ounce Sea Scallops-Cool, Yin tonic
- 1 Egg, Chicken-Neutral, Yin tonic, Blood tonic
- 1 ounce Radish-Neutral, transforms phlegm, drains damp, resolves stagnation
- ½ Pear-Cool, Yin tonic, transforms phlegm
- 1 ounce Spinach-Cool, Yin tonic, Blood tonic
- 1 ounce Sweet Potatoes-Neutral, Qi tonic

1) Wash and peel the fruits and vegetables; cut into bite-sized pieces.
2) Cut the heart into 1" chunks.
3) Rinse the crab meat in a strainer.
4) Place all the ingredients into the slow cooker. Fill the slow cooker with water to cover the food.
5) Place the lid onto the pot, put on low, and simmer for 8-10 hours. You will want to ensure your meat is fully cooked.
6) Remove the egg and peel the shell. Cut the egg into pieces and place in a container or dish. Strain out the water; place the remaining ingredients into the same dish.

509 Calories, Fat 20%, Protein 63%

Seafood Medley

A pleasant meal with a little of everything.
High in blood tonics and foods that help drain damp. Great for pets with dry eye.

- 4 ounces Clam Meat-Cool, Yin tonic, transforms phlegm
- 3 ounces Beef Heart-Neutral, Blood tonic
- 2 ounces Wild Caught Alaskan Cod-Cool, Yin tonic
- 1 Can Sardines In Water-Neutral, Blood tonic
- 3.75 ounces Pumpkin Puree-Warm, Qi tonic, Blood tonic
- 2.5 ounces Mixed Fruit and Vegetables-Neutral
- 1/8 cup dry Brown Rice –Cool, Qi tonic, Blood tonic

1) Wash and peel the fruits and vegetables; cut into bite-sized pieces.
2) Cut the meat into 1" chunks.
3) Place all the ingredients into the slow cooker, except for the pumpkin puree. Fill the slow cooker with water to cover the food.
4) Place the lid onto the pot, put on low, and simmer for 8-10 hours. You will want to ensure your meat is fully cooked.
5) Strain out the water; place the meal in a container or bowl and add the pumpkin puree.

499 Calories, Fat 18%, Protein 48%

Alligator Oatmeal

This meal will really get things moving and shaking.
Filled with delightful Qi and Blood tonics.

- 3.5 ounces Alligator Meat-Cool, Yin tonic
- 4 ounces Pork Kidney-Neutral, Yin tonic, Blood tonic
- 2 ounces Yellow Squash-Cool, Qi tonic
- 1 ounce Strawberries-Neutral, Yang tonic
- 1 ounce Spinach-Cool, Blood tonic
- ½ Apple-Neutral, Yin tonic, transforms phlegm
- .5 ounce Celery-Cool, drains damp
- 1/8 cup dry Steel Cut Oats-Warm, Qi tonic

1) Wash and peel the fruits and vegetables; cut into bite-sized pieces.
2) Cut the kidney into 1" chunks.
3) Place all the ingredients into the slow cooker. Fill the slow cooker with water to cover the food.
4) Place the lid onto the pot, put on low, and simmer for 8-10 hours. You will want to ensure your meat is fully cooked.
5) Strain out the water; place the meal in a container or bowl. The strawberries and oats smell amazing when cooking!
500 Calories, Fat 15%, Protein 55%

Dreaming Of Seafood

A lovely dish that drains damp and is full of Yin and Blood tonics.
Excellent for summer days.

- •2 ounces Alligator Meat-Cool, Yin tonic
- •1 ounce Wild Caught Alaskan Cod-Cool, Yin tonic
- •1 ounce Sea Scallops-Cool, Yin tonic
- •2 ounces Pork Kidney-Neutral, Yin tonic, Blood tonic
- •3 Dates, Seeds Removed-Neutral, Blood tonic
- •.5 ounce Sweet Potatoes-Neutral, Qi tonic
- •.5 ounce Celery-Cool, drains damp
- •.5 ounce Eggplant-Cool
- •.5 ounce Raspberry-Warm, Yang tonic
- •1/8 cup dry Green Lentils-Neutral
- •1/8 cup Red Kidney Beans-Neutral, Yin tonic, Blood tonic, drains damp

1)Wash and peel the fruits and vegetables; cut into bite-sized pieces.
2)Cut the meat into 1" chunks.
3)Place all the ingredients into the slow cooker. Fill the slow cooker with water to cover the food.
4)Place the lid onto the pot, put on low, and simmer for 8-10 hours. You will want to ensure your meat is fully cooked.
5)Strain out the water; place the meal in a container or bowl.
497 Calories, Fat 9%, Protein 48%

Pork & Veggies Fruit Dish

A sweet, neutral meal with hearty Blood tonics.

- 10 ounces Pork Tenderloin-Boneless-Neutral, Yin tonic
- 2 ounces Beef Heart-Neutral, Blood tonic
- 2.5 ounces Mixed Fruits and Vegetables (celery, eggplant, raspberries, carrots, dates)-Neutral
- 1/8 cup dry Brown Rice-Cool, Qi tonic

1) Wash and peel the fruits and vegetables; cut into bite-sized pieces.
2) Cut the meat into 1" chunks.
3) Place all the ingredients into the slow cooker. Fill the slow cooker with water to cover the food.
4) Place the lid onto the pot, put on low, and simmer for 8-10 hours. You will want to ensure your meat is fully cooked.
5) Strain out the water; place the meal in a container or bowl.

502 Calories, Fat 18%, Protein 78%

Thanksgiving Feast

This festive meal is loaded with Qi and Blood tonics.
Excellent for draining damp.

- •6 ounces Turkey Thighs, Skinless, Boneless-Cool
- •2.5 ounces Chicken Hearts-Warm, Blood tonic
- •3 ounces Spaghetti Squash, Cooked-Warm, Qi tonic
- •1 ounce Carrots-Neutral, Blood tonic, resolves stagnation
- •1 ounce Celery-Cool, drains damp
- •½ cup Cranberries-Cool, drains damp
- •1/8 cup dry Steel Cut Oats-Warm, Qi tonic

1)Cut the spaghetti squash in half and bake on cookie sheet in 375 degree oven for 2 hours. After cooling, remove 3 ounces of the squash and place into slow cooker.
2)Wash and peel the fruits and vegetables; cut into bite-sized pieces.
3)Cut the meat into 1" chunks.
4)Place all the remaining ingredients into the slow cooker. Fill the slow cooker with water to   cover the food.
5)Place the lid onto the pot, put on low, and simmer for 8-10 hours. You will want to ensure your meat is fully cooked.
6)Strain out the water; place the meal in a container or bowl. Happy Turkey Day!
499 Calories, Fat 27%, Protein 48%

Pork Stew

This exceptional meal is loaded to the brim with everything good!
Yin, Qi, and Blood tonics, draining properties and it's a mover and shaker.

•10 ounces Pork Tenderloin-Boneless-Neutral, Yin tonic
•1 ounce Beef Liver-Neutral, Blood tonic
•1 Chicken Egg-Neutral, Blood tonic, Yin tonic
•1 ounce Celery-Cool, drains damp
•1 Shiitake Mushroom-Neutral, Qi tonic, drains damp
•1 ounce Sweet Potatoes-Neutral, Qi tonic
•.5 ounce White Radish-Neutral, transforms phlegm, drains damp, resolves stagnation
•.5 ounce Carrots-Neutral, Blood tonic, resolves stagnation
•¼ Pear-Cool, Yin tonic, transforms phlegm
•¼ Apple-Neutral, Yin tonic, transforms phlegm
•1/16 cup dry Wild Rice-Cool, Qi tonic, Blood tonic
•1/16 cup Black Beans-Neutral, Yin tonic, Blood tonic

1)Wash and peel the fruits and vegetables; cut into bite-sized pieces.
2)Cut the meat into 1" chunks.
3)Place all the ingredients into the slow cooker. Fill the slow cooker with water to cover the food.
4)Place the lid onto the pot, put on low, and simmer for 8-10 hours. You will want to ensure your meat is fully cooked.
5)Remove the egg and peel the shell. Cut the egg into pieces and place in a container or dish. Strain out the water; place the remaining ingredients into the same dish.
495 Calories, Fat 19%, Protein 51%

Savory Rabbit

This specialty dish is packed with Qi tonics and foods that drain damp.

• 7 ounces Rabbit, Ground (with organs)-Cool, Qi tonic, Yin tonic
• 1/8 cup Green Lentils, Dry-Neutral
• 1 Garlic Clove-Hot, Yang tonic, drains damp, transforms phlegm, resolves stagnation
• 2.5 ounces Sweet Potatoes-Neutral, Qi tonic
• 1 ounce Asparagus-Warm, Yin tonic, drains damp
• 1 Shiitake Mushroom-Neutral, Qi tonic, drains damp

1)Wash and peel the fruits and vegetables; cut into bite-sized pieces.
2)Peel the garlic clove; mince.
3)Place all the ingredients into the slow cooker, crumbling the rabbit meat over the top. Fill the slow cooker with water to cover the food.
4)Place the lid onto the pot, put on low, and simmer for 8-10 hours. You will want to ensure your meat is fully cooked.
5)Strain out the water; place the meal in a container or bowl.
503 Calories, Fat 12%, Protein 55%

Venison Delight

A great dish full of Blood tonics; good for moving stagnation.

- 4.75 ounces Venison-Warm, Yang tonic, Qi tonic, resolves stagnation
- 3.25 ounces Turkey Heart-Cool, Blood tonic
- ¼ cup Cranberries-Cool, drains damp
- 1 ounce Spinach-Cool, Blood tonic, Yin tonic
- 1 ounce Raspberries-Warm, Yang tonic
- 1 ounce Strawberries-Neutral, Yang tonic
- 1 ounce Radish, White-Neutral, drains damp, transforms phlegm, resolves stagnation
- 1 ounce Asparagus-Warm, Yin tonic, drains damp
- .5 ounce Carrots-Neutral, Blood tonic, resolves stagnation
- .5 ounce Sweet Potatoes-Neutral, Qi tonic
- 1/8 cup dry Quinoa-Warm, Yang tonic

1) Wash and peel the fruits and vegetables; cut into bite-sized pieces.
2) Cut the hearts into 1" chunks.
3) Place all the ingredients into the slow cooker. Fill the slow cooker with water to cover the food.
4) Place the lid onto the pot, put on low, and simmer for 8-10 hours. You will want to ensure your meat is fully cooked.
5) Strain out the water; place the meal in a container or bowl.

501 Calories, Fat 31%, Protein 45%

Fabulous Beefy Clams

A great neutral dish full of everything good!
Lots of good Qi tonics, damp-draining foods, and great for moving stagnation.
Another great meal for dogs with cancer.

- 4 ounces Clams-Cool, Yin tonic, transforms phlegm
- 5 ounces Beef Round-Eye Chunks-Neutral, Blood tonic, Qi tonic
- 1 ounce Beef Heart-Neutral, Blood tonic
- 1 ounce Strawberry-Neutral, Yang tonic
- 1 ounce Radish, White-Neutral, drains damp, transforms phlegm, resolves stagnation
- 1 ounce Raspberries-Warm, Yang tonic
- 1 ounce Sweet Potatoes-Neutral, Qi tonic
- 1 ounce Asparagus-Warm, Yin tonic, drains damp
- ½ Orange-Cool, transforms phlegm
- 1/8 cup Steel Cut Oats, Dry-Warm

1) Wash and peel the fruits and vegetables; cut into bite-sized pieces.
2) Cut the meat into 1" chunks.
3) Place all the ingredients into the slow cooker. Fill the slow cooker with water to cover the food.
4) Place the lid onto the pot, put on low, and simmer for 8-10 hours. You will want to ensure your meat is fully cooked.
5) Strain out the water; place the meal in a container or bowl.
500 Calories, Fat 19%, Protein 49%

Kick'n It Up a Notch Turkey Thighs

A sweet dish packed with Qi and Blood tonics.
Nice for moving stagnation.

- 4 ounces Chicken Thighs, Boneless, Skinless-Warm, Qi tonic, resolves stagnation
- 3 ounces Turkey Thighs, Boneless, Skinless-Cool to Neutral
- 3 ounces Beef Kidney-Neutral, Blood tonic
- 1.5 ounces Turkey Hearts-Cool, Blood tonic
- 1.5 ounces Sweet Potatoes-Neutral, Qi tonic
- ¼ Apple-Neutral, Yin tonic, transforms phlegm
- ¼ Banana-Cool, Yin tonic
- 1/8 cup dry Green Lentils-Neutral, drain damp

1) Wash and peel the fruits and vegetables; cut into bite-sized pieces.
2) Cut the meat into 1" chunks.
3) Place all the ingredients into the slow cooker. Fill the slow cooker with water to cover the food.
4) Place the lid onto the pot, put on low, and simmer for 8-10 hours. You will want to ensure your meat is fully cooked.
5) Strain out the water; place the meal in a container or bowl.

502 Calories, Fat 20%, Protein 54%

Zesty Lobster Tail

A special feast for a dog loving his Qi and Blood tonics.
This meal is a mover and shaker.

- 1 Small Lobster Tail-Warm, Yang tonic
- 14 Mussels-Cool, Yin tonic
- 1.5 ounces Chicken Hearts-Warm, Blood tonic
- 1 ounce Eggplant-Cool
- 1 ounce Cooked Pumpkin-Warm, Qi tonic
- 1 Shiitake Mushroom-Neutral, Qi tonic, drains damp
- 1 Chicken Egg-Neutral, Blood tonic, Yin tonic
- 1/8 cup dry Adzuki Beans-Neutral, drains damp
- Lemon Zest-Neutral, drains damp, transforms phlegm

1)Cut the pumpkin in half and bake on cookie sheet in 375 degree oven for 2 hours. After cooling, remove 1 ounce of the pumpkin meat and set aside.

2)Wash and peel the eggplant; cut into bite-sized pieces. Wash and cut the mushrooms.

3)Place all the ingredients except the pumpkin and lemon zest into the slow cooker. Fill the slow cooker with water to cover the food.

4)Place the lid onto the pot, put on low, and simmer for 8-10 hours. You will want to ensure your meat is fully cooked.

5)Remove the egg and peel the shell. Cut the egg into pieces and place in a container or dish.

6)Remove the meat from the mussels; place in the same dish.

7)Strain out the water; place the remaining ingredients into the same dish, adding the pumpkin and lemon zest. **499 Calories, Fat 26%, Protein 47%**

Sardine Feast

A tasty meal full of Blood tonics.
Great for moving stagnation and draining damp.

- •3 ounce Sardines, Fresh-Neutral, Blood tonic
- •8 Mussels-Neutral, Yang tonic
- •2.5 ounces Chicken Hearts-Warm, Blood tonic
- •2 ounces Kale-Warm, Blood tonic
- •½ Apple-Neutral, Yin tonic, transforms phlegm
- •1/8 cup dry Adzuki Beans-Neutral, Blood tonic, drains damp
- •1 tsp Apple Cider Vinegar-Warm, resolves stagnation

1)Wash and peel the fruits and vegetables; cut into bite-sized pieces.
2)Remove the bones, head, tail, and innards from the sardine; discard them.
3)Place all the ingredients except the vinegar into the slow cooker. Fill the slow cooker with water to cover the food.
4)Place the lid onto the pot, put on low, and simmer for 8-10 hours. You will want to ensure your meat is fully cooked.
5)Strain out the water; place the meal in a container or bowl and add the vinegar.
499 Calories, Fat 18%, Protein 38%

On The Farm

This dish will move stagnation, drain damp, and is chock full of Qi and Blood tonics.

- •4.5 ounces Turkey Thighs, Boneless, Skinless-Cool
- •4 ounces Pork Tenderloin-Boneless-Neutral, Yin tonic
- •1 ounce Buffalo-Neutral, Blood tonic
- •1 ounce Beef Liver-Neutral, Blood tonic
- •1 ounce Celery-Cool, drains damp
- •1 ounce Sweet Potatoes-Neutral, Qi tonic
- •.5 ounce Carrots-Neutral, Blood tonic, resolves stagnation
- •.5 ounce Kale-Warm, Blood tonic
- •¼ Apple-Neutral, transforms phlegm, Yin tonic
- •¼ Orange-Cool, transforms phlegm
- •1/8 cup dry Pearled Barley-Cool, Yin tonic, Blood tonic, drains damp
- •Orange Zest-Warm, resolves stagnation

1)Wash and peel the fruits and vegetables; cut into bite-sized pieces.
2)Cut the meat into 1" chunks.
3)Place all the ingredients into the slow cooker except for the orange zest. Fill the slow cooker with water to cover the food.
4)Place the lid onto the pot, put on low, and simmer for 8-10 hours. You will want to ensure your meat is fully cooked.
5)Strain out the water; place the meal in a container or bowl and add the orange zest.
498 Calories, Fat 20%, Protein 51%

Succulent Duck With Cranberries

Packed full of Qi and Blood tonics, this meal will also move stagnation and help drain damp.

•4 ounces Ground Duck-Cool, Yin tonic

•2.5 ounces Chicken Hearts-Warm, Blood tonic

•¼ cup Cranberries-Cool, drains damp

•1 ounce Beets-Neutral, Blood tonic

•1 ounce Sweet Potatoes-Neutral, Qi tonic

•.5 ounce Green Peppers-Warm, transforms phlegm

•.5 ounce Watercress-Cool, resolves stagnation

•.5 ounce Kale-Warm, Blood tonic

•¼ Apple-Neutral, Yin tonic, transforms phlegm

•1/16 cup dry Basmati Rice-Warm, Qi tonic

•1/16 cup dry Black Beans-Neutral, Yin tonic, Blood tonic

1)Wash and peel the fruits and vegetables; cut into bite-sized pieces.
2)Place all the ingredients into the slow cooker, crumbling the duck on top. Fill the slow cooker with water to cover the food.
3)Place the lid onto the pot, put on low, and simmer for 8-10 hours. You will want to ensure your meat is fully cooked.
4)Strain out the water; place the meal in a container or bowl.
501 Calories, Fat 31%, Protein 37%

Sweet Beef & Fruit

A nice warm meal for a cold day.
This meal is brimming with Blood tonics and foods to drain damp and transform phlegm.

- 8 ounces Ground Beef, 95% Lean-Neutral, Blood tonic, Qi tonic
- 1 ounce Chicken Hearts-Warm, Blood tonic
- 1 ounce Green Peppers-Warm, transforms phlegm
- .5 ounce Radish, White-Neutral, drains damp, transforms phlegm, resolves stagnation
- .5 ounce Kale-Warm, Blood tonic
- .5 ounce Mango-Cool, Yin tonic
- ¼ Banana-Cool, Yin tonic
- ¼ Apple-Neutral, Yin tonic, transforms phlegm
- 1/8 cup dry Red Lentils-Neutral, drain damp
- 1 tbsp Marjoram-Cool, drains damp

1) Wash and peel the fruits and vegetables; cut into bite-sized pieces.
2) Roll the hamburger into 1' balls and place into the slow cooker.
3) Place all the remaining ingredients into the slow cooker and fill with water to cover the food.
4) Place the lid onto the pot, put on low, and simmer for 8-10 hours. You will want to ensure your meat is fully cooked.
5) Strain out the water; place the meal in a container or bowl.
503 Calories, Fat 26%, Protein50%

Not Your Average Pork & Beans

A satisfying neutral meal for any time of the year.
Packed with Qi and Blood tonics and healthy foods to drain excess damp, this is a real hit.

- 5.5 ounces Beef Round-Eye Chunks-Neutral, Qi tonic, Blood tonic
- 1.5 ounces Pork Heart-Neutral, Blood tonic
- 1 Chicken Egg-Neutral, Blood tonic, Yin tonic
- .5 ounce Pumpkin Puree-Warm, Qi tonic
- .5 ounce Celery-Cool, drains damp
- .25 ounce Carrots-Neutral, Blood tonic, resolve stagnation
- .25 ounce Blackberries-Warm, Yang tonic
- ¼ Pear-Cool, Yin tonic, transforms phlegm
- 1/16 cup dry Pearled Barley-Cool, Yin tonic, Blood tonic, drains damp
- 1/16 cup dry Black Beans-Neutral, Yin tonic, Blood tonic

1)Wash and peel the fruits and vegetables; cut into bite-sized pieces.
2)Cut the meat into 1" chunks.
3)Place all the ingredients except the pumpkin puree into the slow cooker. Fill the slow cooker with water to cover the food.
4)Place the lid onto the pot, put on low, and simmer for 8-10 hours. You will want to ensure your meat is fully cooked.
5)Strain out the water; place the meal in a container or bowl and add the pumpkin puree.
6)Remove the egg and peel the shell. Cut the egg into pieces and add to the meal.
499 Calories Fat 26%, Protein 53%

Spanish Mackerel

This meal is packed, packed to the brim with everything good and savory.
A nice warming dish for a chilly day.

- •9 ounces Wild Caught Alaskan Cod-Cool, Yin tonic
- •2 ounces Mackerel-Neutral, Qi tonic, drains damp
- •1 ounce Beef Heart-Neutral, Blood tonic
- •2 Dates-Neutral, Blood tonic
- •1 ounce Celery-Cool, drains damp
- •1 ounce Red Peppers-Warm, transforms phlegm
- •.5 ounce Carrots-Neutral, Blood tonic, resolves stagnation
- •¼ Orange-Cool, transforms phlegm
- •1/16 cup Mung Bean, Dry-Cool, Yin tonic, drains damp
- •1/16 cup dry Steel Cut Oats-Warm, Qi tonic
- •1 Parsley Sprigs-Neutral, Blood tonic, resolves stagnation
- •Lemon Zest-Warm, transforms phlegm
- •1 Garlic Clove-Hot, Yang tonic, drains damp, transforms phlegm, resolves stagnation

1)Wash and peel the fruits and vegetables; cut into bite-sized pieces. Peel and dice the garlic clove.
2)Remove the bones, head, tail, and innards from the mackerel and cod; discard them.
3)Cut the meat into 1" chunks.
4)Place all the ingredients except the lemon zest into the slow cooker. Fill the slow cooker with water to cover the food.
5)Place the lid onto the pot, put on low, and simmer for 8-10 hours. You will want to ensure your meat is fully cooked.
6)Strain out the water; place the meal in a container or bowl and add the lemon zest.
507 Calories, Fat 20%, Protein 54%

Tropical Salmon Delight

This savory dish is full of valuable Qi tonics.
Perfect for a cold night.

- 9ounces Wild Caught Flounder-Cool
- 1.5 ounces Wild Alaskan Salmon-Cool, Blood tonic
- 1ounce Chicken Hearts-Warm, Blood tonic
- 1 ounce Celery-Cool, drains damp
- 1 ounce Carrots-Neutral, Blood tonic, resolves stagnation
- .5 ounce Green Peppers-Warm, transforms phlegm
- .5 ounce Asparagus-Warm, Yin tonic, drains damp
- .5 ounce White Radish-Neutral, drains damp, transforms phlegm, resolves stagnation
- 1/16 cup dry Split Peas-Neutral, Yin tonic
- 1/16 cup Red Quinoa, Dry-Warm, Yang tonic
- 1 TBSP real Coconut Shreds-Warm
- 1 TSP Ground Cinnamon-Hot, Yang tonic

1) Wash and peel the fruits and vegetables; cut into bite-sized pieces.
2) Remove the bones, head, tail, and innards from the flounder and salmon; discard them.
3) Cut the meat into 1" chunks.
4) Place all the ingredients except the coconut and cinnamon into the slow cooker. Fill the slow cooker with water to cover the food.
5) Place the lid onto the pot, put on low, and simmer for 8-10 hours. You will want to ensure your meat is fully cooked.
6) Strain out the water; place the meal in a container or bowl and add the coconut and cinnamon.
494 Calories, Fat 29%, Protein 53%

What's up Doc?

This zesty neutral dish is an all-around good choice for draining damp, resolving stagnation, and transforming phlegm. Nice Qi and Blood tonics to top it off.

•5 ounces Rabbit Meat-Cool, Qi tonic, Yin tonic
•3.5 ounces Goat Lung-Hot, Yang tonic
•1 ounce Carrots-Neutral, Blood tonic, resolves stagnation
•1 ounce Red Peppers-Warm, transforms phlegm
•1 ounce Asparagus-Warm, Yin tonic, drains damp
•.5 ounce Celery-Cool, drains damp
•.5 ounce White Radish-Neutral, drains damp, transforms phlegm, resolves stagnation
•½ Orange-Cool, transforms phlegm
•¼ Apple-Neutral, Yin tonic, transforms phlegm
•1/8 cup Split Peas, Dry-Neutral, Yin tonic

1)Wash and peel the fruits and vegetables; cut into bite-sized pieces. Peel and dice the garlic   clove.
2)Cut the meat into 1" chunks.
3)Place all the ingredients into the slow cooker. Fill the slow cooker with water to cover the food.
4)Place the lid onto the pot, put on low, and simmer for 8-10 hours. You will want to ensure your meat is fully cooked.
5)Strain out the water; place the meal in a container or bowl.
500 Calories, Fat 14%, Protein 55%

Chicken Little Lunch

This meal is packed Blood tonics and is full of draining foods,
topped off with a healthy dose of Qi tonics.

- •5.25 ounces Chicken Breast, Boneless, Skinless-Warm, Qi tonic
- •3.25 ounces Beef Heart-Neutral, Blood tonic
- •1 Chicken Egg-Neutral, Blood tonic, Yin tonic
- •1/8 cup Red Kidney Beans, Dry-Neutral, Blood tonic, Yin tonic, drains damp
- •2 ounces Sweet Potatoes-Neutral, Qi tonic
- •.5 ounces Celery-Cool, drains damp
- •.5 ounces Apples-Neutral, Yin tonic, transforms phlegm

1) Wash and peel the fruits and vegetables; cut into bite-sized pieces.
2) Cut the meat into 1" chunks.
3) Place all the ingredients into the slow cooker. Fill the slow cooker with water to cover the food.
4) Place the lid onto the pot, put on low and simmer for 8-10 hours. You will want to ensure your meat is fully cooked.
5) Strain out the water; place the meal in a container or bowl.
6) Remove the egg and peel the shell. Cut the egg into pieces and add to the meal.
505 Calories, Fat 16%, Protein 59%

Rabbit Buffet

This little dish has it all! High in foods that resolve stagnation, Blood and Qi tonics, and a good helping of foods that drain damp and resolve phlegm.

- •5 ounces Rabbit Meat-Cool, Qi tonic, Yin tonic
- •1 ounces Chicken Hearts-Warm, Blood tonic
- •1 Chicken Egg-Neutral, Blood tonic, Yin tonic
- •2 ounces Raspberries-Warm, Yang tonic
- •1 ounce White Radish-Neutral, drains damp, transforms phlegm, resolves stagnation
- •1 ounce Beets-Neutral, Blood tonic
- •.5 ounce Eggplant-Cool
- •1/8 Apple-Neutral, Yin tonic, transforms phlegm
- •1/16 cup dry Wild Rice-Cool, Qi tonic, Blood tonic
- •1/16 cup Red Kidney Beans-Neutral, Blood tonic, Yin tonic, drains damp

1)Wash and peel the fruits and vegetables; cut into bite sized pieces.
2)Cut the meat into 1" chunks.
3)Place all the ingredients into the slow cooker. Fill the slow cooker with water to cover the food.
4)Place the lid onto the pot, put on low, and simmer for 8-10 hours. You will want to ensure your meat is fully cooked.
5)Strain out the water; place the meal in a container or bowl.
6)Remove the egg and peel the shell. Cut the egg into pieces and add to the meal.
500 Calories, Fat 25%, Protein 48%

Cluck Cluck Moo

This appetizing dish is full of Qi and Blood tonics.
The meal also has a nice dose of foods that drain damp, move stagnation, and transform phlegm.

- 6.5ounces Beef Round-Eye Chunks-Neutral, Blood tonic, Qi tonic
- 1 ounce Turkey Heart-Neutral, Blood tonic
- 1.5 ounces Sweet Potatoes-Neutral, Qi tonic
- 1 Chicken Egg-Neutral, Blood tonic, Yin tonic
- 2 ounces Green Peppers-Warm, transforms phelgm
- 1 ounce Asparagus-Warm, Yin tonic, drains damp
- 1/16 cup dry Black Beans-Neutral, Yin tonic, Blood tonic
- Orange Zest-Warm, resolves stagnation

1) Wash and peel the fruits and vegetables; cut into bite-sized pieces.
2) Cut the meat into 1" chunks.
3) Place all the ingredients except the orange zest into the slow cooker. Fill the slow cooker with water to cover the food.
4) Place the lid onto the pot, put on low, and simmer for 8-10 hours. You will want to ensure your meat is fully cooked.
5) Strain out the water; place the meal in a container or bowl and add the zest.
499 Calories, Fat 26%, Protein 72%

Dexalacarte

High in Blood and Qi tonics, this dish is delightful.
Dexalacarte also has foods to drain damp and move stagnation.

- 6.5 ounces Sea Scallops-Cool, Yin tonic
- 3 ounces Pork Chops, Boneless-Neutral, Yin tonic
- 1 ounce Pork Heart-Neutral, Blood tonic
- 3 ounces Asparagus-Warm, Yin tonic, drains damp
- 2 ounces Carrots-Neutral, Blood tonic, resolves stagnation
- 1.5 ounces Sweet Potatoes-Neutral, Qi tonic
- 1/8 cup dry Basmati Rice-Warm, Yang tonic, Qi tonic, drains damp

1) Wash and peel the fruits and vegetables; cut into bite-sized pieces.
2) Cut the meat into 1" chunks.
3) Place all the ingredients into the slow cooker. Fill the slow cooker with water to cover the food.
4) Place the lid onto the pot, put on low, and simmer for 8-10 hours. You will want to ensure your meat is fully cooked.
5) Strain out the water; place the meal in a container or bowl.
499 Calories, Fat 26%, Protein 44%

Rabbit Deluxe

This meal is great for moving stagnation.
Filled with healthy foods containing Qi and Blood tonics.

•4 ounces Rabbit Meat-Cool, Yin tonic, Qi tonic

•3.75 ounces Goat Lung-Hot, Yang tonic

•2.5 ounces Eggplant-Cool

•1 Chicken Egg-Neutral, Blood tonic, Yin tonic

•.5 ounce Butternut Squash-Pure-Warm, Yang tonic, Qi tonic

•¼ Orange-Cool, transforms phlegm

•1 Shiitake Mushroom-Neutral, Qi tonic, Yin tonic, drains damp

•1/8 cup dry Black Lentils-Neutral, Blood tonic, Yin tonic

•Orange Zest-Warm, resolves stagnation

1)Wash and peel the fruits and vegetables; cut into bite-sized pieces.
2)Cut the meat into 1" chunks.
3)Place all the ingredients except zest into the slow cooker. Fill the slow cooker with water to cover the food.
4)Place the lid onto the pot, put on low, and simmer for 8-10 hours. You will want to ensure your meat is fully cooked.
5)Strain out the water; place the meal in a container or bowl.
6)Remove the egg and peel the shell. Cut the egg into pieces and add to the meal, along with the zest.
501 Calories, Fat 22%, Protein 56%

Dex's Delicacy

This neutral to cool meal is filled with Qi and Blood tonics, along with foods to drain damp.
These make this meal a hit in the summer!

- 4 ounces Rabbit Meat-Cool, Yin tonic, Qi tonic
- 3.75 ounces Goat Lung-Hot, Yang tonic
- 1 Chicken Egg-Neutral, Yin tonic, Blood tonic
- 1 ounce Dates-Neutral, Blood tonic
- 1 ounce Strawberries-Neutral, Yang tonic
- .5 ounce Beets-Neutral, Blood tonic
- ¼ cup Cranberries-Cool, drain damp
- 1/8 cup dry Adzuki Beans-Neutral, Yin tonic, Blood tonic, drain damp

1) Wash and peel the fruits and vegetables; cut into bite-sized pieces.
2) Cut the meat into 1" chunks.
3) Place all the ingredients into the slow cooker. Fill the slow cooker with water to cover the food.
4) Place the lid onto the pot, put on low, and simmer for 8-10 hours. You will want to ensure your meat is fully cooked.
5) Strain out the water; place the meal in a container or bowl.
6) Remove the egg and peel the shell. Cut the egg into pieces and add to the meal.
500 Calories, Fat 19%, Protein 46%

Drool Starter Dinner

This delectable dish is teeming with Qi tonics, Blood tonics, and
foods that resolve stagnation and drain damp.

- 10 ounces Wild Caught Alaskan Cod-Cool, Yin tonic
- 2 ounces Mackerel-Neutral, Qi tonic, drains damp
- 1 ounce Beef Kidney-Neutral, Yang tonic
- 2 ounces Strawberries-Neutral, Yang tonic
- 1 ounce Sweet Potatoes-Neutral, Qi tonic
- 1 ounce Carrots-Neutral, Blood tonic, resolves stagnation
- 1 ounce Asparagus-Warm, Yin tonic, drains damp
- .5 ounce Blueberries-Cool, drains damp
- 1 Date-Neutral, Blood tonic, Qi tonic
- 1/8 cup dry Adzuki Beans-Neutral, Yin tonic, Blood tonic, drains damp
- 1 TSP Ginger, Ground-Warm, Yang tonic, transforms phlegm, resolves stagnation

1)Wash and peel the fruits and vegetables; cut into bite-sized pieces.
2)Remove the bones, head, tail, and innards from the mackerel and cod; discard them.
3)Cut the meat into 1" chunks.
4)Place all the ingredients except the ginger into the slow cooker. Fill the slow cooker with water to cover the food.
5)Place the lid onto the pot, put on low, and simmer for 8-10 hours. You will want to ensure your meat is fully cooked.
6)Strain out the water; place the meal in a container or bowl and add the ginger.
500 Calories, Fat 26%, Protein 28%

Mutter's Stew

A nice neutral dish, chock-full of Qi and Blood tonics.
Bursting with foods to help resolve stagnation and drain damp.

- 7 ounces Beef Round-Eye Chunks Neutral, Qi tonic, Blood tonic
- 1 ounce Beef Kidney-Neutral, Yang tonic
- 2 ounces Carrots-Neutral, Blood tonic, resolves stagnation
- 2 ounces Butternut Squash, Puree-Warm, Yang tonic, Qi tonic
- 1 Date-Neutral, Blood tonic, Qi tonic
- 1/8 cup dry Pearled Barley-Cool, Yin tonic, Blood tonic, drains damp
- 4 Sprigs Marjoram-Cool, Yin tonic, drains damp

1) Wash and peel the fruits and vegetables; cut into bite-sized pieces.
2) Cut the meat into 1" chunks.
3) Place all the ingredients into the slow cooker. Fill the slow cooker with water to cover the food.
4) Place the lid onto the pot, put on low, and simmer for 8-10 hours. You will want to ensure your meat is fully cooked.
5) Strain out the water; place the meal in a container or bowl.
500 Calories, Fat 19%, Protein 54%

Pork & Beans

A simple and satisfying dish with all the tonics and draining properties tossed in.

•8 ounces Pork Tenderloin-Boneless-Neutral, Yin tonic
•2.25 ounces Chicken Hearts-Warm, Blood tonic
•3 ounces Celery-Cool, drains damp
•½ Banana-Cool, Yin tonic
•1/8 cup dry Mung Beans-Cool, Yin tonic, drains damp

1)Wash and peel the fruits and vegetables; cut into bite-sized pieces.
2)Cut the meat into 1" chunks.
3)Place all the ingredients into the slow cooker. Fill the slow cooker with water to cover the food.
4)Place the lid onto the pot, put on low, and simmer for 8-10 hours. You will want to ensure your meat is fully cooked.
5)Strain out the water; place the meal in a container or bowl.
503 Calories, Fat 21%, Protein 54%

Zesty Chicken

A wonderful selection of foods high in Qi and Blood tonics, along with foods that resolve stagnation and transform phlegm.

- 7.25 ounces Chicken Breast, Boneless, Skinless-Warm, Qi tonic
- 3.75 ounces Pork Kidney-Neutral, Yang tonic
- 3 ounces Red Peppers-Warm, transforms phlegm
- 2 ounces Carrots-Neutral, Blood tonic, resolves stagnation
- ½ Pear-Cool, Yin tonic, transforms phlegm
- 1/8 cup dry Brown Rice-Cool, Qi tonic, Blood tonic
- Lemon Zest-Warm, resolves stagnation

1) Wash and peel the fruits and vegetables; cut into bite-sized pieces.
2) Cut the meat into 1" chunks.
3) Place all the ingredients into the slow cooker except the zest. Fill the slow cooker with water to cover the food.
4) Place the lid onto the pot, put on low, and simmer for 8-10 hours. You will want to ensure your meat is fully cooked.
5) Strain out the water; place the meal in a container or bowl and add zest.
500 Calories, Fat 12%, Protein 56%

Smorgasbord Stew

This meal is robust with lots of flavors to tempt any dog. Filled with Qi and Blood tonics, along with foods to resolve stagnation and drain damp, it's a great meal.

•6.5 ounces Chicken Thighs, Boneless, Skinless-Warm, Qi tonic
•3.25 ounces Beef Heart-Neutral, Blood tonic
•2.5 ounces Celery-Cool, drains damp
•2 ounces Asparagus-Warm, Yin tonic, drains damp
•2 ounces Carrots-Neutral, Blood tonic, resolves stagnation
•½ Apple-Neutral, Yin tonic, transforms phlegm
•1/8 cup dry Wild Rice-Cool, Qi tonic, Blood tonic

1)Wash and peel the fruits and vegetables; cut into bite-sized pieces.
2)Cut the meat into 1" chunks.
3)Place all the ingredients into the slow cooker. Fill the slow cooker with water to cover the food.
4)Place the lid onto the pot, put on low, and simmer for 8-10 hours. You will want to ensure your meat is fully cooked.
5)Strain out the water; place the meal in a container or bowl.
500 Calories, Fat 22%, Protein 50%

Beefy Delight

Fresh, fast, and easy dish filled with Qi and Blood tonics, along with
foods to move stagnation and drain damp.

•7 ounces Ground Beef 95% Lean-Neutral, Qi tonic, Blood tonic
•2 ounces Beef Liver-Neutral, Blood tonic
•1 Chicken Egg-Neutral, Yin tonic, Blood tonic
•1/8 cup dry Pearled Barley-Cool, Yin tonic, Blood tonic, drains damp

1)Wash and peel the fruits and vegetables; cut into bite-sized pieces.
2)Cut the meat into 1" chunks.
3)Place all the ingredients into the slow cooker and crumble the ground beef on top. Fill the slow cooker with water to cover the food.
4)Place the lid onto the pot, put on low, and simmer for 8-10 hours. You will want to ensure your meat is fully cooked.
5)Strain out the water; place the meal in a container or bowl.
6)Remove the egg and peel the shell. Cut the egg into pieces and add to the meal.
500 Calories, Fat 31%, Protein 50%

Beef Eaters

A scrumptious selection of Qi and Blood tonics, along with foods that drain damp and transform phlegm. This hardy dish is the bomb!

•6.5 ounces Beef Round-Eye Chunks-Neutral, Blood tonic, Qi tonic
•1 ounce Beef Liver-Neutral, Blood tonic
•2 ounces Celery-Cool, drains damp
•½ Apple-Neutral, Yin tonic, transforms phlegm
•¼ Banana-Cool, Yin tonic
•1/8 cup dry Black Lentils-Neutral, Blood tonic, drain damp

1)Wash and peel the fruits and vegetables; cut into bite-sized pieces.
2)Cut the meat into 1" chunks.
3)Place all the ingredients into the slow cooker. Fill the slow cooker with water to cover the food.
4)Place the lid onto the pot, put on low, and simmer for 8-10 hours. You will want to ensure your meat is fully cooked.
5)Strain out the water; place the meal in a container or bowl.
498 Calories, Fat 18%, Protein 55%

Move Over Slow Cooker......

In these recipes, we get a little more fancy in our preparation and cooking. After you mastered the slow cooker, you might find that you are looking for something new to try. Remember, these are just suggestions, and substitutions are always an option! Get creative in the kitchen; your dog will love you for it!

Beef Meat Loaf

This is not your average meatloaf!
Full of foods to help drain damp, along with a good dose of Blood tonics.

- 4 ounces Ground Beef 95% Lean-Neutral, Qi tonic, Blood tonic
- 2 ounces Beef Heart-Neutral, Blood tonic
- 2 ounces Tomato-Cool, Yin tonic
- 2 ounces Celery-Cool, drains damp
- 1.5 ounces Green Peppers-Warm,   transforms phlegm
- 1 ounce Shiitake Mushroom-Neutral, Qi tonic, drains damp
- 1 ounce Spinach-Cool, Blood tonic, Yin tonic
- 1 Chicken Egg White-Cool, Qi tonic
- 1 ounce Sweet Potatoes-Neutral, Qi tonic
- 1/8 cup Green Lentils, Dry-Neutral, drain damp

1) Preheat oven to 350 degrees.
2) Wash and peel the fruits and vegetables; cut into bite-sized pieces, saving 6 thin slices of tomato.
3) Place the lentils and 1.5 cups of water into a sauce pan with a lid and bring to a boil. Reduce heat to low and place lid ajar a bit so it doesn't boil over. Cook for 30-45 minutes, or until soft.
4) Cut the meat into 1" chunks.
5) Place all the ingredients except the slices of tomato into a food processor or blender. Puree until smooth.
6) Place mixture into a small loaf pan or muffin pan.
7) Add the tomato slices to the top. Bake in oven for approximately 1 hour, or until done.
503 Calories, Fat 23%, Protein 54%

Buffalo Meatloaf

A nice, neutral dish for any day

A good mixture of food to drain damp and resolve stagnation, along with Blood and Qi tonic foods.

- 6 ounces Ground Beef 95% Lean-Neutral, Qi tonic, Blood tonic
- 1 ounce Buffalo-Neutral, Blood tonic
- ounce Beef Heart-Neutral, Blood tonic
- 1 ounce Sweet Potatoes-Neutral, Qi tonic
- 1 Chicken Egg-Neutral, Blood tonic
- .5 ounce Celery-Cool Yin tonic
- .5 ounce Tomato-Cool, Yin tonic
- ¼ Banana-Cool, Yin tonic
- 1/8 cup dry Wild Rice-Cool, Qi tonic, Blood tonic

1) Preheat oven to 350 degrees.
2) Wash and peel the fruits and vegetables; cut into bite-sized pieces, saving 6 thin slices of tomato.
3) Place the rice and 1.5 cups of water into a sauce pan with a lid; bring to a boil. Reduce heat to low and place lid ajar a bit so it doesn't boil over. Cook for 30-45 minutes, or until soft.
4) Cut the meat into 1" chunks.
5) Place all the ingredients except the slices of tomato into a food processor or blender. Puree until smooth.
6) Place mixture into a small loaf pan or muffin pan.
7) Add the tomato slices to the top. Bake in oven for approximately 1 hour, or until done.
505 Calories, Fat 33%, Protein 45%

Qi Tonic Meatloaf

A nice, neutral dish for any day full of Blood and Qi tonic foods.

- 7 ounces Ground Beef 95% Lean-Neutral, Qi tonic, Blood tonic
- 1 ounce Beef Liver-Neutral, Blood tonic
- 2 ounces Butternut Squash-Pure-Warm, Yang tonic, Qi tonic
- 1 Pear-Cool, Yin tonic, transform phlegm
- 1 ounce Carrots-Neutral, Blood tonic, resolves stagnation
- 1 ounce Blueberries-Cool, drains damp
- 1 Egg, Chicken-Neutral, Yin tonic, Blood tonic

1) Preheat oven to 350 degrees.
2) Wash and peel the fruits and vegetables; cut into bite-sized pieces.
3) Cut the liver into 1" chunks.
4) Place all the ingredients into a food processor or blender. Puree until smooth.
5) Place mixture into a small loaf pan or muffin pan.
6) Bake in oven for approximately 1 hour, or until done.
506 Calories, Fat 25%, Protein 41%

Puppins

A nice, neutral dish for any day full of Blood and Qi tonic foods.

- •7 ounces Ground Beef 95% Lean-Neutral, Qi tonic, Blood tonic
- •2 ounces Beef Liver-Neutral, Blood tonic
- •1 Apple-Neutral, Yin tonic, transforms phlegm
- •2 ounces Asparagus-Warm, Yin tonic, drains damp
- •1 ounce Celery-Cool, drains damp
- •1 ounce Eggplant-Cool
- •1 Egg, Chicken-Neutral, Yin tonic, Blood tonic

1)Preheat oven to 350 degrees.
2)Wash and peel the fruits and vegetables; cut into bite-sized pieces.
3)Cut the liver into 1" chunks.
4)Place all the ingredients into a food processor or blender. Puree until smooth.
5)Place mixture into a small loaf pan or muffin pan.
6)Bake in oven for approximately 1 hour, or until done.
501 Calories, Fat 30%, Protein 48%

Meals to Go and Snacks

These recipes are great for traveling or on the go. Whether you want a meal to fit in your pocket for training or traveling, or you need to cook up something fast on vacation these can fill that need. Extra recipes are provided at the end for snacks and treats to keep on hand for the well deserving pup.

Dehydrated Alligator Trail Mix

A supreme meal for when you are on the go.
This will get your dog's day moving by moving stagnation.

•3.25 ounces Alligator Meat-Cool, Yin tonic
•3.5 ounces Pork Kidney-Neutral, Yang tonic
•3 ounces Sweet Potatoes-Neutral, Qi tonic
•1 Banana-Cool, Yin tonic

1)Wash and peel the fruits and vegetables; cut into 1" x 2" strips, 1/4" thick.
2)Slice meat into 1" x 2" strips, 1/4" thick.
3)Place all the ingredients on dehydrator trays, close to each other but do not overlap.
4)Set dehydrator between 145-155 degrees Fahrenheit for a minimum of 6-12 hours.
5)Once the food is sufficiently dry, take out the bites and place them on a clean surface. With a paper towel, pat off excess natural oils; allow to cool. To check to see if the food is done, attempt to bend it in half. If it bends and doesn't crack, it needs more time. If it breaks in half it's just right.
6)Break the sweet potato chips into tiny bite sized pieces for easier digestion.
500 Calories, Fat 12%, Protein 50%

TIP: The banana will usually finish first. Feel free to remove the bites as they finish dehydrating.

Dehydrated Scallops & Tidbits

A mouth-watering meal that can double as high-value training treats.
Qi tonics, Blood tonics, and foods to move stagnation and drain damp; this dish has it!

• 10 ounces Sea Scallops-Cool, Yin tonic
• 3.25 ounces Beef Heart-Neutral, Blood tonic
• 3.5 ounce Tomato-Cool, Yin tonic
• 3 ounces Sweet Potatoes-Neutral, Qi tonic
• 3 ounces Carrots-Neutral, Blood tonic, resolves stagnation
• 3 ounces Strawberries-Neutral, Yang tonic
• 2 ounces Red Peppers-Warm, transforms phlegm

1) Wash and peel the fruits and vegetables; cut into 1" x 2" strips, 1/4" thick.
2) Slice meat into 1" x 2" strips, 1/4" thick.
3) Place all the ingredients on dehydrator trays, close to each other but do not overlap.
4) Set dehydrator between 145-155 degrees Fahrenheit for a minimum of 6-12 hours.
5) Once the food is sufficiently dry, take out the bites and place them on a clean surface. With a paper towel, pat off excess natural oils and allow to cool. To check to see if the food is done, attempt to bend it in half. If it bends and doesn't crack, it needs more time. If it breaks in half it's just right.
6) Break the sweet potato chips, carrots, and red peppers into tiny bite sized pieces for easier digestion.
501 Calories, Fat 11%, Protein 54%

TIP: Some items will dehydrate quicker than others. Feel free to remove the bites as they finish dehydrating.

Chicken Jerky Dinner

A perfect dish for those dogs who like to munch on their food.
Incredibly tasty Qi and Blood tonics, along with foods to drain damp and move stagnation.

- 7.25 ounces Chicken Breast, Boneless, Skinless-Warm, Qi tonic
- 3.25 ounces Turkey Heart-Neutral Blood tonic
- 2.25 ounces Sweet Potatoes-Neutral, Qi tonic
- ¼ Apple-Neutral, Yin tonic, transforms phlegm
- 1/8 cup Mung Beans, Dry-Cool, Yin tonic

1) Wash and peel the sweet potatoes and apple.
2) Dice meat and veggies into small pieces.
3) Place all the ingredients into a sauce pan. Add water to cover the food at least 2 inches. Bring to a boil.
4) Place lid ajar a bit so it doesn't boil over; reduce heat to low. Cook for 45-60 minutes, or until mung beans are soft.
5) Place all cooked ingredients into a food processor or blender. Puree until smooth.
6) Form into 3" flat discs; place on dehydrator trays, close to each other but do not overlap.
7) Set dehydrator between 145-155 degrees Fahrenheit for a minimum of 8 hours.
8) Once the food is sufficiently dry, take out the cookies and place them on a clean surface; allow them to cool. To check to see if the food is done, attempt to bend it in half. If should snap in half like a soft treat.

496 Calories, Fat 13%, Protein 59%

TIP: This meal can be given as is, or placed in a bowl with warm water to rehydrate.

Coconut Bites

A perfectly healthy treat for a good dog.
Great for resolving stagnation and transforming phlegm.

- ½ Cup Coconut Flour-Warm
- 1 Orange-Cool, transforms phlegm
- 1 Banana-Cool, Yin tonic
- Lemon Zest-Warm, transforms phlegm

1) Preheat oven to 275 degrees Fahrenheit. Line a cookie sheet with parchment paper.
2) Wash and peel the fruits. Chop the banana and orange into bite sized pieces.
3) Place the orange and banana into a food processor or blender. Puree until smooth.
4) Combine your blended fruit and coconut flour; mix well.
5) Form into 3" flat discs; place on lined cookie sheet about 2" apart.
6) Add lemon zest to the uncooked treats.
7) Bake in oven 25-35 minutes or until golden on the bottom.
8) Remove cookies and place them on drying rack to cool.
Approximately 20 cookies, 20 calories each, Fat 24%, Protein 13%

TIP: Keep a few treats in an air-tight container and the remaining treats in the freezer.

Meatball Bites

These warming dog treats are a fantastic Qi tonic!
Extra meaty and delicious for even the most finicky dog.

•10 ounces Ground Beef 95% Lean-Neutral, Qi tonic, Blood tonic

•4 ounces Green Peppers-Warm, transform phlegm

•2.5 ounces Kale-Warm, Blood tonic

•3 Figs-Neutral, Blood tonic, Qi tonic

•1 cup Quinoa Flour-Warm, Yang tonic

•1 tbsp Virgin Coconut Oil-Warm

1)Preheat oven to 275 degrees Fahrenheit. Line a cookie sheet with parchment paper.

2)Wash the peppers and kale. Remove the seeds from the figs. Chop into bite-sized pieces.

3)Pre-heat a frying pan on medium heat for three minutes; add the coconut oil. Move the oil around the pan with a spatula to coat the pan evenly.

4)Add the hamburger; stir fry until almost fully cooked. Add the peppers, kale, and figs to the ground meat. Continue to stir fry until the kale is reduced.

5)Allow the mixture to cool. Once cool, place the mixture into a food processor or blender. Puree until smooth.

6)Combine your blended mixture with the quinoa flour; mix well.

7)Form into 3" flat discs and place on lined cookie sheet about 2" apart.

8)Bake in oven 25-35 minutes or until golden on the bottom.

9)Remove cookies and place them on drying rack to cool.

Approximately 24 cookies, 44 calories each, Fat 29%, Protein 31%

TIP: Keep a few treats in an air-tight container and the remaining treats in the freezer.

Resources

➤**Judy Morgan D.V.M.**

    ➤www.facebook.com/JudyMorganDVM

    ➤Clayton Veterinary Associates 820 North Delsea Drive-Clayton, NJ 08312 (856)881-7470 www.Claytonvetnj.com

    ➤www.youtube.com/user/DrJudyMorgan

➤**Tonya Wilhelm**

    ➤www.Globaldogtrainer.com

    ➤www.facebook.com/toledodogtraining

    ➤www.youtube.com/toledodogtraining

➤**Dexter The Dog**

    ➤www.Dexterthedog.com

    ➤www.Vacationswithyourdog.com

Printed in Great Britain
by Amazon